S0-FPI-464

HOW TO EARN MORE THAN

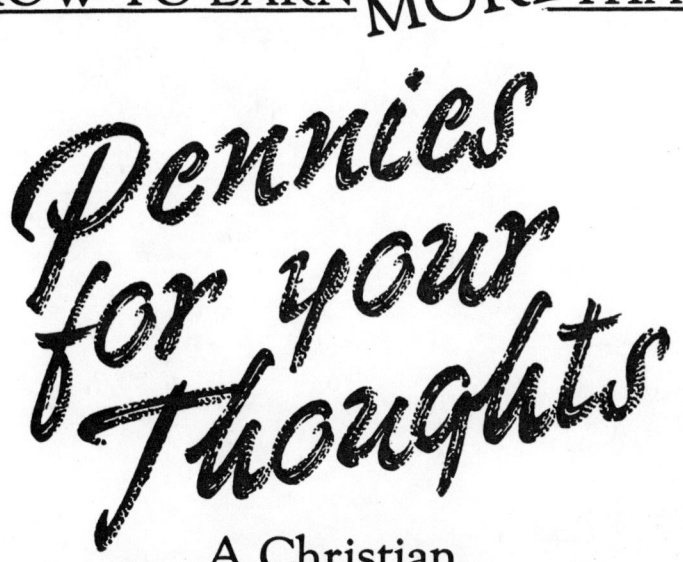

Pennies for your Thoughts

A Christian Writer's Guidebook

Holly G. Miller

**Warner Press, Inc.
Anderson, Indiana**

All scripture passages, unless otherwise indicated, are from the King James Version ©1972 by Thomas Nelson or the Revised Standard Version ©1972 by Thomas Nelson.

Copyright ©1990 by Warner Press, Inc.
ISBN 0-87162-501-6
All Rights Reserved
Printed in the United States of America
Warner Press, Inc.
Arlo F. Newell, Editor in Chief
Dan Harman, Book Editor
Cover by Debbie Apple
Stock #D4318

Contents

Here's Holly.. vi
Introduction vii

Chapter	Title	Page
1	How To Boost Your Productivity	1
2	The Four Hottest Nonfiction Markets...........	13
3	Checklist: 13 Thou Shalt Nots	27
4	Quick Starts, Fast Finishes	31
5	500 Words about 500-Word Sidebars	47
6	Sourcery and Popping the Questions...........	51
7	Writing from Your Own Experience.............	67
8	The Truth about Fiction	81
9	Selling Yourself and Your Ideas................	93
10	Cut the Noise	107
11	How to Get There from Here	119
12	P.S. On Promoting Self	133

Glossary: Coming To Terms With Writing 139
Notes... 149

Here's Holly

Holy G. Miller is a name you should know by now. She's a former Senior Editor of Saturday Evening Post, but she burst on the national scene with outstanding interviews with such prominent figures as George Burns, Erma Bombeck and Julio Iglesias. Then she moved to ghost writing for some national personalities (her "autobiographies" have made some famous people even more famous).

Holly has an MA in journalism from Ball State U and is presently a professor of journalism at Anderson U in Indiana. She travels widely and has gathered in some impressive awards, including ones from the Associated Press, the National Federation of Press Women and the Evangelical Press Association.

Holly writes under her own name and a string of pen names. One of her favorites is Leslie Holden, a name attached to great fiction and a pseudonym for the joint efforts of Holly and her co-author, Dennis Hensley.

Holly and her husband Phil live in Anderson, IN and are cheering their two sons, Charles and Whitney, as they complete their college careers.

Introduction

I love to "do lunch" with editors.

I enjoy hearing them rehash their war stories, dream out loud about what they'd like to see from us free-lancers, and grouse about what they hope they'll never see again. I love listening as they debate future cover topics, trade industry insights, and bemoan the status of their slush. (Sorry, but "slush" is slang for unsolicited submissions.) Such shoptalk not only benefits my own free-lance career, but serves as a market report for me to pass along to participants in the writing workshops I conduct around the country.

Recently I flew to Chicago to lunch with the managing editor of a Christian women's magazine. I had completed an article for her December issue, and she had suggested that I deliver it personally. The trip had several purposes—it's not common practice to ask a writer to trek two hundred miles with manuscript in hand—and I was delighted to accept the invitation.

This was to be a get-acquainted session. The magazine had moved its headquarters from the East Coast to the Midwest a few months earlier, and a new staff had been recruited. I was asked to hop the red-eye from Indianapolis, spend the day meeting with the editors, trading ideas for future issues, and, yes, socializing over lunch.

I waited until dessert before popping my first question.

"How are we doing?" I began, bluntly, leaning over my strawberry cheesecake. "How good are the manuscripts that come in unannounced from us free-lancers? Are we making progress?"

She paused, then flashed me a "so-so" gesture with her hand.

"That bad, huh?"

"It's changing," she said between bites.

"Getting better?" I prodded. Another pause. She seemed to be struggling to frame the right response.

"It used to be so easy to spot beginners," she offered at last. "Their manuscripts were generally handwritten on mauve stationery, folded six times, and stuffed into envelopes that smelled like rosewater. And they never included return postage."

"And now?"

"Now it's different. Maybe it's because of all the writers' workshops, the 'how-to-write' books, and the writers' magazines. Now the submissions are flawlessly formatted, meticulously typed, carefully weighed, and have stamps neatly tucked under paper clips. Now we have to read the manuscripts to know how bad they are."

She was right.

Writers of Christian material have changed in recent years, and editors of Christian publications have changed, too. I'm only sorry one hasn't kept pace with the other. Contemporary editors no longer are past pastors who made midlife moves into publishing as a reward for service or as an escape from burnout. Today's editors are trained journalists, armed with strategic business plans, demographic studies, and high expectations. They're industry executives, and they expect us writers to be the same. We may not need their academic degrees, but we have to share their dedication. Publishing is their profession as well as their ministry.

Christian editors have changed because Christian readers have changed. Today's readers are savvy, demanding, and busy. They want to be stretched, not stroked. They prefer authors who teach, not preach; they like writers who offer application rather than recitation of scripture. They want fiction that is wholesome, not contrived; advice books that contain answers, not platitudes; and articles that are timely, not trite.

As Christian writers we have to know readers' demands and know how to meet them. Our manuscripts must *be* sharp as well as look sharp. To succeed in Christian publishing we have to be more than good Christians; we have to be good Christian communicators. If a double standard ever existed—one set of writing rules for secular writers and an easier set for Christian writers—it no longer applies. Editors are looking for great writers who can produce a great deal of great material on assignment and on time. If we can't do it, they'll find others who can. They'll turn to the secular ranks where the pros know how to churn out prose. Give these secular writers a topic, inspirational or otherwise, and they'll produce a salable manuscript every time.

This book will help you do the same.

But first a word of warning: The chapters that follow are geared to serious writers who are willing to change old habits and refine new skills. They will help beginning writers break into print, published writers expand their markets, and veteran writers increase their earnings. Experience and education are of little concern. Whether or not you are a part-time or a full-time writer isn't important. What really counts is if you are a determined writer.

Our emphasis will be on learning to communicate well and delivering the message in creative new packages. We'll talk about such important topics as writing from your own experience, selling yourself and your ideas to editors, and avoiding the thirteen errors that lead to rejections. We'll also discuss uncomfortable issues: what to charge for your articles, how to promote yourself, and how to draw attention to what you've said. We'll even offer some pointers on manuscript preparation so you won't be tempted to revive the rosewater or press the pink stationery back into service.

Where do we begin? By finding the time to write.

Let's get organized. . . .

1

How to Boost Your Productivity

TIME MANAGEMENT expert Alan Lakein estimates that most people waste eighty percent of their time. They may look busy, says Lakein, but that's because they haven't cut the clutter from their days.[1] They're active, but they're not always productive. Often they lack goals and are guilty of procrastination. It's no wonder so many of them complain that they have no time to do what they really want to do.

Like write.

Most writers are procrastinators. Even authors who seem to be phenomenally productive and have byline credits to prove it, admit to needing a nudge on occasion. A good example is William Sydney Porter, better known as O. Henry, who wrote sixty-six short stories in 1904 alone. His output dwindled the following year, however, and by December of 1905 he had nearly stopped writing all together. He was tired, the words weren't flowing, and his editors at the *New York Sunday World* were worried that he would renege on his commitment to create something special for their Christmas edition.

The content of New York newspapers was different in those days, and fiction was a favorite—particularly the fiction of O. Henry. For that reason, *World* editors had been delighted when they had convinced him to produce a suitable story for the holidays. Delight turned to panic, though, when the day before his deadline came and he still had submitted nothing.

A young staff reporter was dispatched to find the writer and to apply some gentle pressure on him. Since the reporter was in awe of the popular O. Henry, he kept his distance after locating the author in a tiny neighborhood cafe. The two men sat in different booths eyeing each other. Finally, well into the evening, O. Henry nodded to the reporter that it was time to leave. They walked the short distance to O. Henry's apartment where the reporter stretched out on the sofa, and the writer began scrawling the opening lines of his story. As pages were completed they were given to a delivery boy to carry to the anxious editors waiting downtown.

By morning, millions of New Yorkers were marveling at O. Henry's latest gift to them. Readers still take joy in its poignancy and beauty. "The Gift of the Magi," first published that Christmas season, has become a tradition, told and retold on the printed page, on the stage, and on film. It may have been written in hours, but its impact has been felt for ages.

Are you a procrastinator? If so, you're in good company. The advantage that a published writer has over the beginner is a pressure to produce. The veteran works on assignment and is given a deadline by the editor. Deadlines can be great motivators. The novice, on the other hand, rarely works on assignment and is spared the burden (and incentive) of knowing someone is waiting for the submission. No one inquires about her progress, no one nudges her for a first draft, and no one scolds her for tucking the opening paragraphs into the bottom drawer until her next surge of creativity. Certainly no one sends an envoy to sit across from her at a neighborhood cafe to stare her into action.

When you're a beginner, you have to put pressure on

yourself to be productive. How? Here are ten ways to do it.

1. PICK YOUR POCKETS

Everyone has them. They're those little blocks of time, often only minutes, that are wedged between commitments. They can add up, though; just ask Ken Taylor, former director of Moody Press and founder of Tyndale House Publishers, Inc.[2]

For years Ken Taylor commuted from his home in Wheaton, Illinois, to his office in downtown Chicago. It was an hour each way, or ten hours a week, or forty hours a month. Rather than napping or reading the paper on his trips to and from the city, Ken would prop his briefcase on his knees and write. His project was personal and geared to his family. His ten young children were struggling to understand the scripture they were reading as part of evening devotions. To boost their comprehension, Ken spent his hours on the train paraphrasing the verses.

From these pockets of time—two hours a day, ten hours a week, forty hours a month—came a manuscript. Seven years after he first began jotting words on a pad at his makeshift desk on the train, he had produced *Living Letters*. This later evolved into the *Living Bible*, the nation's topselling book for 1972 and 1973. More than 33 million copies are currently in circulation, and the *Living Bible* has been translated into ten languages, while the *Living New Testament* is available in fifty.

If Ken Taylor used his pockets of time well, so did Marabel Morgan, an unlikely best-selling author whose book *The Total Woman* sold three million copies in paperback and 638,000 in hardcover edition. Marabel is the first to admit that she's no writer, and at the time she wrote *The Total Woman* her time was totally taken by a preschooler and a newborn. Still, her Christian advice book (how to replace fizzle with sizzle in a marriage) was the number-one blockbuster of 1974. I interviewed her once for a *Writer's Digest* article, and my first question was as much for myself as for my readers.

"How did you do it?" I wanted to know.

"Fifteen-second snatches," she replied. "I wrote *The Total Woman* on yellow legal sheets, scribbled and pasted together during intervals between caring for our four-year-old daughter and our baby."[3]

She couldn't even type and was so insecure about her talent that she asked her editor if he would lose his job if *The Total Woman* were a total failure. To save face and perhaps his position, she bought three hundred copies of the first press run and stashed them in her garage. She needn't have worried. The book and all of its sequels are still selling well.

Pockets of time. Snatches. Intervals. What you label them is less important than what you do with them.

2. JUST SAY NO

Two summers ago I was on the faculty of the Cape Cod Writers' Conference, Inc., at Craigville, Massachusetts. Among my duties was to consult privately with young writers who mailed in advance their short manuscripts for my critique. The conference director warned me that one author had requested a meeting but had refused to send her work. Instead, she had promised to bring her submission with her. I would have to do my best to look it over and comment on it during our one-on-one session.

At the appointed hour I looked out the window of my temporary office and, to my surprise, saw an elderly woman with a suitcase laboriously making her way up the walk.

"I'm your one o'clock appointment," she said in lieu of an introduction.

"And this must be—?" I nodded to her bulging suitcase.

"My book," she confirmed, heaving it onto my desk. I reviewed a few pages—there were hundreds—and gave her a quick assessment. Her story was inspiring but it needed to be revised and cut by half. Why not sign up for my workshop class? I suggested. The lectures would help her as she prepared a second draft.

"I don't have time," she replied.

"What's your hurry?"

"I'm seventy-seven."

I didn't ask her why she had waited so long to write her story; I already knew the answer. I had heard it before from dozens of writers who, like she, had waited too long to get started.

Christian writers have an obligation to view their writing as their ministry. We write instead of—not in addition to—organizing the women's luncheons, running the church rummage sale, and serving on the curriculum committee. Writing is our unique contribution to the work of the church. People may make us feel guilty about our "hobby"; they may even belittle it, try to talk us out of it, and lure us away from it. Even if they indulge us and acknowledge our pastime, they'll never understand it.

If you are pressed to defend what you do, try this: In 1986, a nationwide test was given to determine what seventeen-year-olds know. These were high school juniors from every type of background—boys, girls, urban, rural, black, and white. Two thirds of them could not identify Job, and the same number had never heard of Sodom and Gomorrah.

Where are the Christian communicators?

When your friends approach you with yet another volunteer job, tell them that you already have a job, a big one, and then just say no.

3. PUT CHAINS ON YOUR BIKE

This piece of advice is directed at published writers who are dissatisfied with their markets and discouraged by the infrequency of their bylines. They feel the same frustration as did a young journalist from North Manchester, Indiana, who contacted me several years ago about a job. I was managing editor of a daily newspaper at the time, and although I had no openings on my staff, I hired him anyway. Why? Because of the creative letter that accompanied his résumé.

"I'm working on a very small weekly newspaper," he wrote. "I'm grateful for the job, but it's a lot like riding a bicycle without a chain. I'm getting lots of practice, but I'm not going anywhere."

Many Christian writers can identify with this. They're writing a lot, but they're writing the same kind of material for the same kind of publications. They're not moving forward. They're treading water, running in place, riding a bike without a chain. They're producing words, but they're not reaching new audiences with them.

To be successful, you've got to stretch. Don't be a writer who says, "I don't do fiction"; "I don't do scripts"; "I don't do curriculum lessons"; "I don't do profile articles." Be a writer who does it all. Put a chain on your bike and take off in new directions.

4. KNOW THE WORLD YOU WANT TO CHANGE

One of the most productive and successful Christian writers of recent years is Gloria Gaither. She's a poet, has published more than five hundred songs, has written six books, is a contributing editor to *The Christian Herald,* has won a Grammy, and was chosen Gospel Songwriter of the Year in 1985.

Gloria once said during an interview[4] that she and her husband/collaborator Bill keep a little black book of ideas. Call it a journal, a vest-pocket ledger, or a "tickler file," it serves as a repository of "maybes" that someday may be set to music or may be recycled in book or story form. Most of the ideas are words, phrases, and observations pulled from the Gaithers' busy lives as parents of three, residents of a rural community, and overseers of a worldwide ministry.

The productivity tip to be gleaned from Bill and Gloria Gaithers' success is this: Learn to blend your worlds. Don't waste valuable time shedding the burdens and frustrations of everyday life in order to withdraw and write on loftier levels. Instead, write about your burdens and frustrations. Use them to relate to your readers, to provide a timeliness to your topic, and to illustrate key points.

Successful Christian writers are active participants and observers of today. They know the world they want to change. They write with familiarity because they selectively sample the music and media of the secular and Christian marketplace in order to do business there. This doesn't mean they must read materials that are offensive to them, but they're aware of the issues that are out there and of the answers that others have provided. Then they offer alternatives; they contribute the Christian perspective.

"What's a nice, middle-aged mother of three doing reading *Rolling Stone?*" I once asked Gloria Gaither as a follow-up to my request for a list of publications she regularly reads. She answered my question with one of her own.

"How can my lyrics have an impact on young people unless I know what else is influencing them?" she said. "I need to know my competition if I'm to give listeners a choice."

5. SET OUTPUT GOALS

Most writers set measurable goals to boost their productivity. Some set word goals, others prefer time goals, and a few, like Ernest Hemingway, have devised unique yardsticks to gauge their output. "Papa" Hemingway, according to the story, believed that when he had worn down seven number-two pencils, that was a good indicator of a productive day. (How that translates into keystrokes at a word processor is anyone's guess.)

If you like the idea of setting a daily word goal, a reasonable number is five hundred words of polished copy. As writing becomes more of a habit and less of a hobby you may find your goal isn't aggressive enough. At that point, increase the quota to a thousand words a day. Adhere to your goal, and avoid writing yourself dry one day and not writing at all the next. Stop while you still feel enthusiasm—that way you'll look forward to picking up the action in the next session. Stop midway through a thought or chapter—that way you'll know where you're going the next time you roll the paper into your typewriter or boot up your computer.

6. COMB YOUR HAIR

Productive writers put on their shoes. And comb their hair. And splash a little Georgio on their wrists. This advice comes highly recommended from Virginia Muir, longtime managing editor and colleague of Ken Taylor at Tyndale House. What Jinny means is this: If you plan to produce a great deal of great copy, you've got to approach writing as a serious business. You've got to keep regular hours (even if they're only part-time hours); take short, planned breaks, and hold personal calls to a minimum.

How long would you last in an office if you shuffled in once or twice a week in your bathrobe, snapped on the radio, flipped through your files, yawned twice, and went to bed? Silly question, perhaps, but a lot of writers operate in such a haphazard way.

When you work at home, it's easy to become too casual about your appearance. This casualness can spill over to your work habits and finally to your work. Call it a quirk, but I always dress for phone interviews. The person I'm interviewing can't see me, so I am judged by my voice and my manner. Both must exude confidence and professionalism. If I am to act as a professional, I have to feel like a professional. That means I have to look like a professional. Sweats and Reeboks will never do.

So put on your shoes, comb your hair, hold your calls, and get to work.

7. BECOME A JUGGLER

Most productive writers have at least three projects in

progress at any given time. Isaac Asimov, author of more than 350 books, divides his talents among six or seven assignments at once. He has a personal collection of 3,000 volumes so he doesn't have to stop writing to go to the library. When asked what he would do if his doctor told him he had only a few months to live, he replied that he wouldn't give up or brood; he'd merely type faster. Now, that's a man with a mission.

Juggling several diverse writing projects simultaneously can boost your output. One project will refresh you for another. If your enthusiasm diminishes for an assignment that requires in-depth research, your energy picks up when you turn to a piece of fiction for teenagers. If progress on an article grinds to a halt because a key interview can't be scheduled for several days, you merely direct your attention to a project that has no such obstacles.

The secret of making this multi-project concept work is two-fold. First, the projects should represent real variety. A good mix might include fiction, non-fiction, a bit of humor, and a piece of poetry. Make sure the potential audiences for your works are as varied as your topics. Perhaps your how-to article is geared to readers of a woman's magazine; the fiction might be directed to children, and the novel could be appropriate for a general audience. This variety of readers will cause you to shift your tone (breezy? chatty? factual? serious?), adjust your vocabulary upward or downward, and shorten or lengthen your sentences and paragraphs. It will keep you alert.

Second, when you're juggling three or four projects at once, make sure each one is at a different stage of development. Perhaps you're gathering background information for a historical novel, writing a first draft of a short story, making final corrections on a personality interview, and attempting to market a collection of verse. When you achieve that kind of a blend, one project can provide a rejuvenating change of pace from another. If you burn out on the first, you can fire up with the second.

8. CONSIDER COLLABORATION

If writing is a rat race, turn it into a relay by forming a partnership with another author. By choosing your collaborator carefully, you can sometimes double your productivity. Success will depend completely on your pick of a partner. Here are a few guidelines.

- Join forces with a writer who has skills, background, or expertise that you lack. You don't need a clone but rather a complement to your own talent.
- Make sure there is time and commitment to do fifty percent of the work. Otherwise, resentment will result.
- Agree to disagree in a professional manner. Partners have to tolerate each other's criticism.
- Find someone who is on your writing level. A joint project will be uneven if one partner is a veteran and the other is a novice. Your goal is seamless writing with no obvious breaks in style.

When Dr. Dennis Hensley and I collaborated on a series of Christian novels under the pen name of Leslie Holden, we were able to complete three books in less than two years. The reason we were so productive was that we worked separately, but simultaneously, on different chapters, and we drew from two sets of personal experiences: his and mine. I could write knowledgeably about our major female character, an executive based in Detroit, because I had worked in public relations at General Motors for four years. Dennis could write comfortably about our key male character, a POW in Vietnam, because like our hero, Dennis had been stationed in Vietnam during his tour of duty with the army.

Many collaborations end in dispute. Resentment builds, squabbles result, and friendships disintegrate. Depending on the partners' personalities, writing partnerships can mean half the work or twice the trouble.

9. KNOW WHEN TO LET GO

It's been said that a productive writer never gift-wraps the garbage. What that means is this: Don't get bogged down in unnecesary details. Don't do more than you have to do. Giving 100 percent is great, but don't give 110 percent if you don't have to, and if nobody cares one way or another.

I know writers who conduct interviews and then go back to their offices with their tape recorders and transcribe word-for-word everything that was said during the conversation. They may only be planning to use one or two quotes, but they transcribe on paper every hiccup and sneeze.

I know writers who won't release their manuscripts until their spouses, relatives, friends, ministers, and high school English teachers all have passed affirmative judgment on them. They make every change that every reader prescribes until their work isn't theirs at all. What results is an article or short story written by committee.

I know writers who, if they find a typo as they edit their final manuscript, insist on retyping a new page. Draft after draft passes through their printers as old mistakes are corrected and new ones created.

Know when to let go. Polishing and refining your work is fine—up to a point. After that, reworking a manuscript actually can have an adverse effect. Overcorrecting can drain away style and deplete freshness. Several versions later you may be reinstating words and phrases that you deleted earlier. Revision or indecision: which does the editing reflect? Maybe it's time to slip the dog-eared pages into their plain brown wrapper and leave the decision to the editors.

10. KNOW WHAT'S HOT, WHAT'S NOT

I have a friend, Gene Policinsky, who is an assistant managing editor of *USA Today*. (The publication has been called the McNewspaper of the '80s; you know it by its bright colors, short articles, and huge weather map.) A newcomer on the journalism scene—it debuted in 1982—*USA Today* already is the most widely read daily newspaper in the country. The secret of its success? Gene offers this explanation: "We give our readers news they can use," he says.

Christian writers can take a cue from *USA Today*. We, too, need to give our readers news they can use. By doing this we increase our number of sales, decrease our number of rejections, and boost our level of productivity. The truly productive writer doesn't waste time creating material that will never be published. He knows what readers want to read and what publishers want to publish. In short, he knows what's hot and what's not.

Not long ago I enjoyed a banner month in which I tallied three major sales to three major Christian publishing houses. The first sale was a magazine article about women workaholics; the second was a proposal for a book about anxiety; the third was an article about senior citizens not acting their age in the 1980s. (I'll tell you more about that one later.) You might think, But those aren't Christian topics. Exactly! They aren't traditional Christian topics. They're contemporary topics to which I gave a Christian twist. And that's why they sold.

How do you know what's hot and what's not? It's a matter of tuning into the times and determining the cares, concerns, and interests of the reader. Chapter Two will highlight four sure-fire categories of nonfiction that fulfill all criteria. Read on. . . .

2

The Four Hottest Nonfiction Markets

NOBODY SHOCKS an audience better than Van Varner, editor of *Guideposts Magazine*. Imagine this You're sitting in a classroom at the Writing Institute in Denver, Colorado, anxiously awaiting the man who makes editorial decisions at the undersized magazine with the oversized circulation (twelfth largest in the country, at 4.5 million subscribers). A self-described curmudgeon, Varner meanders to the podium, frisks himself in search of his 3-by-5 note cards, peers out at the packed houseful of aspiring writers, and begins to tick off guidelines for writing *Guideposts* stories.

"Lesson number one," he growls at the group. "Forget God."

Members of the audience pause, mid-scribble, to look around nervously at each other. Did he say what they thought he said? Surely not. A hand shoots up in the air to request that the speaker repeat himself, please. Varner agrees, consults his card, and says it again.

"Forget God."

How do you follow a line like that? Very quickly, in this case.

"Think story," explains Varner. "Stories are about conflict, change, and crisis. *Guideposts* stories tell how people overcome conflict. God is in every one of us, and he's there during a crisis. As writers, you should think first about your story, because if you tell your story well, your readers will see God in it."

Good advice. I was in the audience that afternoon and joined the rest of the workshop participants in applauding Van's shoot-from-the-hip approach.

Effective Christian articles and stories don't tell about God's presence, but *show* God's presence instead. For this reason, most editors of inspirational publications aren't looking for "Christian articles," but rather contemporary articles told from a Christian point of view. The four most salable subjects in the Christian marketplace also are among the most salable in the general press. The difference is in the treatment, and the treatment had better be subtle, not heavy-handed. Hard sell won't sell.

Right now, *the hottest, most easy-to-market categories of nonfiction are issues, profiles, calendar-related articles, and wellness.* Each category contains thousands of potential stories that can inspire, inform, entertain, influence, and instruct readers. Let's look at the categories separately, beginning with the one that is currently most in demand—**issues.**

What's Happening?

"Roe v. Wade: Are We Ready For Its Reversal?"

"Why More Moms Are Opting To Home School Their Kids."

"New Help For The Homeless."

"Baby Boom Or Baby Bust—A Look At Parenting In the '90s."

"Runaway Teens: A Growing Concern In Suburbia."

These topics, provocative by some standards, would be equally at home between the covers of *US News and*

World Report or *The Christian Herald.* They're contemporary, they touch a lot of people, they deal with social issues and moral values, and some are downright controversial. The best way to tackle any one of them is by using a *round-up approach.* Here's how it works: Take an issue of public concern, rephrase the issue into question form, identify an assortment of people who might have good information to share on the question, ask these people to reply to your question, and then compile their responses.

Let's take an example.

The topic: The Homeless in America

The question: What is being done by the Christian community to help the homeless in America?

Respondents: Pastors of urban churches; spokespersons for denominations; directors of inner-city missions and outreach ministries: representatives of community service organizations.

The answers provided by the respondents will be the "meat" of the article. Mixed in with these answers will be numbers and facts—easily attainable at the library—that estimate how many homeless persons live on the streets of America, how the number has grown in the past five to ten years, which cities are most affected by the problem, what the government has done to curb and address the dilemma, and a summary of new proposals under consideration (studies, legislation, pilot programs).

Such an article, as in-depth as it is, could easily be researched on the telephone, through correspondence, and at the local library. Yet it probably would be welcomed by most editors at most inspirational magazines. The Christian twist is provided in two ways: first, by the angle selected (what the Christian community is doing about the homeless in America); and, second, by the sources surveyed (pastors, missions, directors, and the like).

To have success in writing issues-related articles, you obviously have to keep up with what's happening. This involves constantly monitoring the media (secular and Christian) and knowing which issues are being covered by journalists and broadcasters and which are being aired on discussions/talk shows (again, secular and Christian). You need to tune in to how Christians are reacting to and coping with these hot issues.

Timing is everything. Most topics have life cycles. People are fascinated by new subjects, but their interest wanes after they've been saturated with information on the topics. Excitement can only be revived if fresh material is uncovered or if something happens to make the topic suddenly timely again.

Take abortion, for instance. In 1973, when the Roe v. Wade decision legalized abortion, a glut of articles, opinion pieces, surveys, and reaction stories resulted. Everyone had something to say about abortion, and said it. But as time passed and interest diminished, the number of articles also diminished. Finally, a regularity set in. The topic surfaced only at an anniversary ("Five years after Roe v. Wade...," "Ten years after the legalization of abortion....") or when a pro-life march on Washington thrust the issue into the headlines again.

The subject became worthy of additional in-depth treatment when President Reagan named several new justices to the U.S. Supreme Court and it seemed possible that if the abortion issue were reconsidered, Roe v. Wade might be reversed. Suddenly the topic, ho-hum for several years, was hot again.

Still, a writer needs an angle. Dean Merrill, editor of *The Christian Herald,* suggested this one to me: If abortion were no longer an option, is the church ready to help provide all the services that pregnant women need? It's one thing for Christians to support the pro-life position, but are they willing to offer housing, counseling, adoption services, parenting classes, and medical care for mothers-to-be who have nowhere to turn?

Interesting questions. I decided to approach the assignment as a round-up story. Is the church ready for a

Roe v. Wade reversal? In the reference area of the public library I located telephone directories from several major cities. By checking the Yellow Pages, I came up with the names, addresses, and phone numbers of an assortment of Christian agencies that reach out to troubled pregnant women. I was careful not to select organizations located in the same part of the country, but chose one in New Jersey, another in Texas, a third in Pennsylvania, a fourth in Missouri, a fifth in Indiana, and a sixth in Washington, D.C.

While at the library, I did some quick research to update myself on the general topic of abortion. I knew I would have to include in my article a lot of background information. For instance, I wanted to know how many abortions are performed in a year (about 1.6 million); I wondered about the typical candidate for abortion (she's unmarried, less than twenty-five years old, frequently poor and nonwhite, has had a previous abortion in two out of five cases); and I was curious about how the nine members of the Supreme Court viewed the issue (a 4-4 split with the position of one member unknown).[5]

Armed with this information, I was ready to go home and begin calling the six agencies around the country to ask for specifics on what services they provided, how many women they could accommodate in their facilities, their rate of occupancy in the years of legalized abortion, and what problems they foresaw if Roe v. Wade were reversed. When I had completed my telephone interviews, the article was relatively easy to write. My only challenge was in deciding which information to include. I had more than I could use!

Although the two examples I've cited—the homeless in America and abortion—were researched and written by the round-up method, other approaches work equally well. A topic such as the homeless could be looked at not by surveying sources around the country, but rather by focusing on one inner-city church and its efforts to ease the homeless problems in its own neighborhood. The church might serve as a microcosm—a colorful illustration—of what many churches are doing. Blended into the story would be background information about the situation on a national level.

The article that probed Christians' willingness and readiness to help pregnant women could be told from the standpoint of two rural Pennsylvania residents, Jim and Anne Pierson, who have operated Christian maternity homes for several years. In the course of my research for *The Christian Herald* I spoke by phone with this couple and easily could have made them the main focus of my story. In fact, the Piersons have been the topic of many other articles in many other magazines.[6]

When the emphasis of a story is on one person or two people, it generally is called a **profile article,** which is the second easiest-to-market category of nonfiction. Let's take a closer look.

The Case for a Balanced Case

If you've ever had your picture snapped by a professional photographer, you've endured the pain of reviewing the set of unretouched proofs that resulted. Every tiny facial line, freckle or cowlick was captured in living color. The assurance by the photographer that all imperfections would be softened in the finished product did little for your ego. The truth is, no one is perfect, and every once in a while we come face to face with that fact.

The camera doesn't lie, and neither should the pen. A profile article written by a professional writer is very similar to a portrait taken by a professional photographer. The result is an honest likeness of a person as she or he appears to be at a particular moment in her or his life. It isn't altered or fictionalized.

What about all those imperfections? In the case of a verbal picture the "flaws" aren't facial lines, freckles, and cowlicks, but are normal personality shortcomings that everyone shares and shows to some extent. They should neither be ignored nor emphasized in the article. Readers look for themselves in the people they read about, and they like to identify with the strengths and weaknesses of their heroes. They find it difficult to relate to people who have their lives in perfect order and who never struggle with problems. The writer, like the photographer, may choose to soften the imperfections, but she doesn't remove them. If she did, the resulting portrait would be dishonest and would lack credibility.

A profile article is not a biography of a person. It doesn't start with her or his birth and document all of the person's accomplishments. We leave that sort of detail to résumé and obituary writers. As magazine journalists, we concentrate on the one or two aspects of the person that make her or him interesting to the public. Our subject doesn't have to be a celebrity, but he or she must be noteworthy in some way for some reason.

Whereas a round-up article is based on several short interviews with an assortment of people, material for a profile article is usually drawn from one intensive interview with the person who is the subject of the story. To add depth and variety, the writer might want to conduct a couple of brief "support" interviews with friends or associates of the subject. These additional people will contribute their insights from their unique points of view. Think of it this way: Try to imagine a television documentary that is filmed with only one stationary camera. After a while, the documentary becomes static and predictable. Other cameras, looking at the subject from different angles and different distances can add interest and variety. Support interviews can do the same for an article.

Profile stories are a staple of all magazines. Some are short and superficial (five hundred to eight hundred words), and some are long and detailed (two thousand-plus words). Traditionally, most magazines feature the pictures of well-known persons on their covers with profile articles about those persons on the inside pages. All profile articles, however, don't have to be cover stories, and they certainly don't have to be about celebrities. Some of the most inspiring profiles ever written have introduced readers to ordinary people who are involved in extraordinary circumstances.

Much of the success of the profile story depends on two factors—the author's ability to identify interesting subjects to profile and her or his skill in conducting good interviews with those subjects. We'll talk more about the art of choosing subjects and popping questions in Chapter Six.

Well-Seasoned Ideas

After issues-related and profile articles, the easiest type of nonfiction to sell is the **calendar story.** By this I mean any article tied to a season, a holiday, a special observance or an anniversary. Most editors of inspirational and secular publications try to include in each issue at least one article or short story linked to the calendar. What they don't want to see are such tired topics as "What Christmas Means To Me," "The First Thanksgiving," and "The History of Flag Day."

Often editors and writers are extremely creative in how they relate the calendar to an article. For example, a May/June issue of *Campus Life* offered a guide to (very) odd summer jobs for teen-agers; *Christianity Today* ran an editorial about Israel on the eve of that country's fortieth birthday; *Presbyterian Survey* explained how one old slave church in Bucks County, Pennsylvania, celebrates Easter; a writer for *Today's Christian Woman* pooled ideas on what a family can do when it is snowbound for an evening or two (a January/February offering).

Once you tune into the idea of calendar-related articles you see them everywhere. An April issue of *CITY* magazine had no less than three such stories listed in its table of contents. The cover featured a man dressed in court jester costume (April fool) to promote an inside article on what makes people laugh; another story was called "Civil Rights: Twenty Years After the Death of Dr. King," and a third article took readers behind the scenes of local television news shows to see if such telecasts are really as dramatic as those depicted in the Hollywood film "Broadcast News." (The calendar tie-in? "Broadcast News" was nominated for Best Picture of the Year and the Oscar presentation was scheduled for early April.)

Often a calendar story is also either issues-related or is a profile of a person. For instance, *U.S. News and World Report* used the fifteenth anniversary (calendar) of Roe v. Wade as a reason to publish a cover story called "Abortion: America's New Civil War" (issue). The regional magazine *Indianapolis Woman* ran a cover story on Sandi Patti (profile) and titled it "Sandi Patti's Life of Thanks-Living" for a November issue (calendar).

As is true with most articles, good timing is essential to calendar stories. Publications usually work on a three- to six-month lead time. This means that in December when you're decking the halls and wrapping the gifts, editors are thinking about summer travel, Easter celebrations, and spring planting. Not only must you take lead time into consideration, but you also should allow several weeks for correspondence to be exchanged between you and an editor. Generally it works this way: You will submit an article idea (query); the editor will reply favorably; you will research, write, and submit the article; then the editor will read, circulate, and accept the manuscript; you will respond to the offer, and the editor will schedule it for publication. This process can take weeks. To be safe, think about Christmas in June, summer in January, spring in September, and autumn in April.

Here's what I do . . .

Toward the end of each July I sit down and make a twelve-square grid of the upcoming calendar year. My first entries on the grid are predictable. Christmas is always going to be December 25, Independence Day will always be celebrated on July 4, and Thanksgiving always falls on the fourth Thursday of November. Then, with the help of an almanac, I add the "movable" observances such as Easter, Palm Sunday, Ash Wednesday, and Memorial Day. I jot down general, seasonal thoughts: New Year's resolutions, June weddings, summer travel, back to school, winter doldrums. Of course I don't want to forget "people" days such as Mother's Day, Father's Day, Secretary's Day, Grandparents' Day, Valentine's Day. Then there are religious holidays other than the ones my family observes—Passover, Yom Kippur, Hanukkah, and Rosh Hashanah. When gift calendars become available in the stores (usually in late fall), I buy one that has special notations printed next to certain dates: election day, Winter Olympics, income tax deadline, Arbor Day, Super Bowl Sunday, Mardi Gras.

The secret, of course, is to come up with creative ideas to link to certain times of the year. Subtlety helps. Here are three from my files.

- I once wrote an article called "Different Drummer" that explored how military schools were making star-spangled comebacks among parents who wanted their children to be exposed to old-fashioned discipline, God, and patriotism. It was published in a fall (back-to-school) issue of a regional magazine.
- Another article celebrated the thirtieth anniversary of Project HOPE, the world's first peace-time hospital ship. Although the ship was dry-docked several years ago, the treatment-teaching mission goes on. The story was so dramatic that I'll probably revive it on the thirty-fifth and fortieth anniversaries of HOPE.
- I once interviewed a pastor who counts among his flock many of America's top race-car drivers. He always attends the Indianapolis 500-Mile Race, is known as the "preacher of the pits," and is welcomed in the private garage areas where few people are admitted. Since the Indy 500 is called the Memorial Day Classic, I was able to sell the article to a magazine for its May edition.

Enough war stories. By now your head should be spinning with article ideas on issues to explore, people to profile, and dates to commemorate. But wait, there's one more "hot" category that deserves special mention.

Here's to Your Health (and Fitness)

The fourth most salable article category in the Christian marketplace is anything related to **health** (mental, physical, and spiritual), wellness, fitness, feeling and looking good. While health, in general, could come under the umbrella category of issues, it's so broad and has generated so much interest that it occupies an area all its own.

One key reason wellness is a good topic is that the American population is graying. Right now, the life expectancy in the U.S. is about seventy-five years, and twelve percent of our citizens are over the age of sixty-five. Both numbers are expanding. Americans are looking better, feeling healthier, and living longer. And they're turning to books and magazines to help them accomplish this. As with issues articles, profiles, and calendar-related stories, health topics have become magazine mainstays. The good news for free-lancers is that they can write such material without any special training; in fact, some editors prefer that their writers not have an M.D. as part of their bylines. Doctors often struggle to come down to the level of readers. The exception to this advice would be a regular medical column such as that formerly written by Dr. Robert Henry for *Christian Life* ("Feeling Good") or the advice column, "Ask the Briscoes," written by counselors Stuart and Jill Briscoe for *Charisma.*

To succeed in the specialized area of writing health articles for Christian publications, you must first be aware of its scope. Diet and fitness books now account for nine percent of all hardcover book sales. But nutrition and exercise aren't the only hot health subjects these days. Wander through a Christian bookstore and take note of the titles: *AIDS and the Positive Alternatives, Dying for a Drink* (alcoholism), *The Exodus Diet Plan, How to Win Over Depression, How to Beat Burnout.* The same variety you see in books is evident in magazines.

No topic is off limits as long as it is treated tastefully and honestly.

What skills must be developed to write effectively about wellness issues? I asked that question of several health/fitness authors and here's what they said:

- Recognize trends early. "Get your ideas at the newspaper stage," suggested Cameron Stauth, a Eugene, Oregon, free-lancer and former editor of the *Journal of Health Science*. Issues discussed in magazines are generally three- to six-months old and have lost their freshness. So don't depend on them to keep you up-to-date on what's new. Cameron clips newspaper reports of medical breakthroughs and notes who's conducting the studies and where the research is taking place. Other sources that he taps include medical trade publications available through the National Institute of Health.

Karen Cain, a health special in Syracuse, New York, stressed the importance of getting on the mailing lists of professional organizations and support groups such as the American Academy of Pediatrics, the American Heart Association, and the American Cancer Society. Locally, hospital and medical center public relations departments produce newsletters, press releases, brochures, and fact sheets that provide a continuing update on what's new.

"Ideas come from patients, health-care professionals, other publications, and my own experience," said Karen. "For example, I once did an article on how working mothers cope with sick children. I had received a news release from a pediatrics group in Chicago, had read material about sick child centers located in other parts of the country, and as a mother, I had dealt with the problem myself."

- Gain access to experts. For national magazines, the experts you quote must have widespread professional clout. Cameron Stauth starts with a local physician, asks for references and then works up and out. When approaching a medical school faculty, he asks for the head of a department, a full professor, a chief of staff, or someone who's been published on the topic. The U.S. government provides additional contacts through the National Health Information Clearinghouse.

• Humanize scientific data. "The health article that catches my eye deals with the human element rather than the medical," said Nancy Comiskey, former magazine editor and now a writer for a large newspaper in Indianapolis.

To prevent articles from becoming antiseptic, a writer should include anecdotes, brief case histories, and interviews with victims. But be aware that the human element is sometimes tougher to track than the clinical data. Victims may not want to talk, writers can get caught up in the story's emotion, and it's always a tug-of-war between what's warmly personal and what's intimately private.

• Shade articles toward a particular audience. Knowing a magazine's demographics helps accomplish this. For instance, I've written several articles on AIDS, and although the facts don't change, some facts are more appropriate for some audiences. When I write for an adult Christian audience I might emphasize the threat of the AIDS virus being transmitted by a tainted blood supply. When I write for a youthful audience I might mention the more common modes of transmission and the importance of choosing a celebate, drug-free lifestyle.

When Dr. Ken Cooper collected his modest $2,000 advance for his now-classic *Aerobics* in 1968, he had no idea that the book and its sequels would tally 17 million sales worldwide and would set off a fitness boom. Dr. Cooper more recently has turned to wellness (his latest: *Controlling Cholesterol*) because he sees preventive medicine as the next "hot" topic. Since he has a very good track record (pardon the fitness pun) maybe we should follow his lead.

Whatever topic the Christian writer chooses—issues, profile, calendar, or wellness—several obstacles can get in the way. We'll look at thirteen of the most common hurdles in Chapter Three.

3
Checklist:
13 Thou Shalt Nots

OBVIOUSLY, Sally Stuart—former markets columnist for *The Inspirational Writer* magazine, author of more than seven hundred religious articles and twelve books, and compiler of the *Inspirational Writers' Market Guide* —is an expert at selling to Christian publications. That's why her advice is so sobering. When asked how long a writer must work before she or he regularly sees the words (and byline) in print, Sally replied that ten years is a realistic estimate. Ten years, or longer.[7]

It's called "paying your dues," and an aspiring writer can go broke doing it. Happily, there are shortcuts.

Editors reject manuscripts for dozens of reasons. Knowing those reasons and avoiding them can shorten the "dues-paying" period considerably. Of course, some rejections are out of a writer's control. For instance, if an author proposes a story idea and the editor already has the same story in the works, the author's idea will be vetoed. If an editor has a large inventory of articles in the file awaiting publication, he or she may call a halt to any new acquisitions until the inventory is more manageable. Again, the writer who proposes new material will be sent a rejection. If an editor, within the previous two years, has bought and published an article similar to that proposed by an author, that editor probably won't do another version for at least twelve months. (Because of turnover in subscribers, most magazines will consider repeating a topic after three years.) Unfortunately, writers often have no way of distinguishing one reason for rejection from another. Editors can't take time to explain, and so they rely on generic "thanks-but-no-thanks" slips to bear the bad news.

It may be a cop-out to assume that your manuscript was rejected because of circumstances beyond your control. Most material is vetoed simply because it fails to meet editors' standards. Here's a checklist—otherwise known as the unlucky thirteen—of what I call the "thou shalt nots" of free-lance writing. The next time one of your manuscripts fails to earn an editor's nod, ask yourself if you were guilty of one of these all-too-common errors. If none applies, perhaps your manuscript was good but your timing wasn't. Try another market.

Thou shalt not . . .

☐ Revive tired topics. It's best if you can find a topic that hasn't been done to death, but if you're taking another look at a familiar subject, make sure you have a fresh slant to add new life.

☐ Take a broad brush. Since most inspirational magazines prefer articles and stories between fifteen hundred and two thousand words, avoid subjects that are too important to be covered in that abbreviated length. Select a small piece of the big picture and analyze.

☐ Forget the takeaway value. Readers want to extract from your words something they can apply in their lives. Turn your writing inside out. Instead of dwelling on a personal experience such as "My First Christmas as a Widow," turn it around, call it "How to Cope with a Blue Christmas," and emphasize what readers can do if they find themselves in circumstances similar to those you endured.

☐ Sacrifice facts for opinion. Unless you're an expert on a topic and have great credibility, keep your opinions to a minimum. Sharing personal perspectives with readers is great if you support your feelings with weighty evidence. Research is the key.

☐ Ignore the new and the who. Editors and readers want new topics told in people terms. Rather than explaining in clinical jargon a new wonder drug to help depression, talk about the person who developed the medication and the victims who will be helped by it.

☐ Tap sources who aren't credible. If you're writing a story about missionary work in Haiti, don't quote your next door neighbor who visited Port-au-Prince for a day and a half ten years ago. Strive for the best sources with the most impact.

☐ Stop with one source. Lively articles pit the insights and opinions of several people against each other. Plan to quote many persons with divergent points of view.

☐ Write in bloated style. Remember that most publications are written at about eighth or ninth grade level. A warm, conversational style will grab and hold your readers' attention.

☐ Choose topics of limited interest. Ask yourself, Does this subject appeal to women and men? singles and married couples? old and young? Editors want articles that will interest as many readers as possible.

☐ Limit yourself to nostalgia. Most editors prefer material that looks to the future rather than dwells on the past. Exceptions are some speciality publications geared to older persons (*Senior Edition* in Denver, Colorado, will send you its month-by-month breakdown of nostalgia themes if you send editor Allison St. Claire a self-addressed-stamped envelope).

☐ Send wrong material to wrong magazine. If a publication doesn't use any fiction, it's a waste of time and money to send short stories to that market. If an editor has a policy that dictates no first-person opinion pieces, he's not likely to discard his policy just for you. Careful market analysis can cut your rejection rate drastically.

☐ Overlook humor. Much more subtle than one-liners and jokes, humor can take the form of anecdotes, illustrations, and quotes that spark a smile. Whether the purpose of your writing is information, instruction, inspiration, or entertainment, you will accomplish it better with a light touch and a soft style.

The most serious of all shortcomings is lackluster writing in general. This is writing that is gramatically correct, perfectly punctuated, topically important, and boring as all get out. There is no excuse for it. With some 750,000 words at our disposal (English has the largest vocabulary of any language in the world), we need only master the choosing and stringing together of words to evoke the feeling and reaction we want. How do we do this? For openers, let's start with openers.

4

Quick Starts, Fast Finishes

BORING.

Someone once said there is no such thing as a boring topic, only boring writers. I agree. This may be especially true in the Christian marketplace where stimulating subjects too often are rendered yawn-inspiring and snore-inducing under the heavy pen of overzealous writers.

Editors have stopped being Mr. Niceguys when it comes to telling us writers to shape up. Van Varner, who receives about one thousand manuscripts a week at *Guideposts*, says he hates "soft writing" that is laced with words such as *love, heart, tears,* and (his least favorite), *share*. Dean Merrill says the taboo words around *The Christian Herald* offices are *should, need to, ought,* and *we must*. The editors at *Presbyterian Survey* are more general, pointing to "language or syntax too technical or difficult" as quick grounds for rejection.

What's the alternative?

Brightness. Readability. Style. And it should be obvious from the first paragraph. Norman Vincent Peale once complained that the trouble with new writers is their inability to grab readers' attention in the opening lines.[8] He commiserated with the novices and admitted that composing lead paragraphs of a first chapter is his toughest challenge, too. He likened it to opening a bottle of olives. After you've decided how to get the first one out, the others are easy.

The purpose of this chapter is to show you how to write quick starts and fast finishes. In other words, how to get out the olive, serve it with style, and make your readers hungry for more. But first you need to understand the three steps leading to the writing step. I follow this multi-step process whenever I write Christian articles. It's simple, and, more importantly, it works. Briefly:
1. Distill an idea to coverline size.
2. Complete prewriting activities (PAT).
3. Gather research.
4. Write.

Again, Step Four—the writing step—is what we'll stress, but the previous three steps are essential to Step Four's success.

What's Your Handle?

Call it a quirk, but I have to have a title for my article or short story before I begin writing it. A creative, succinct title not only will set the tone of the piece, but will prevent me from getting off track and taking detours into territory I had no intention of exploring. A good title is like a handle; it gives you something to hold onto until the substance is added. It gives your work an identity. The article's value will come later, depending on the quality of the material you pour into it.

Great titles double as great coverlines. Editors depend on coverlines in the same way that a theater manager depends on words posted on her marquee. They catch the eye and interest of passersby and beckon them to come and see what's inside. Coverlines serve the same purpose. They are those sometimes poignant, punchy or provocative words arranged on both sides of a magazine's cover that reach out and grab the passerby. They promise answers to questions and solutions to problems.

If I can't reduce my article idea to a three-to-five-word coverline, my topic probably is too broad. I need to focus it even more tightly. When I'm satisfied that I've distilled the idea to a manageable size that can be covered in-depth in two thousand words, I write the coverline/title on an index card and slip it into the file that I have created for the project. Before I'm done, the file will be bulging with notes, clippings, and copies. All will be related to those few words on the index card.

Pondering PAT

Often an article idea will stay in incubation in my head for several weeks. As I carry it around with me I try to determine the exact purpose of the article, its intended audience, and the tone I plan to use when I write it. Knowing the purpose, audience, and tone (PAT) will help me as I begin to gather research material and when I finally start putting words on paper.

My purpose will probably be a combination of several. My primary goal will be to inspire, but secondary goals may be to inform, entertain, instruct or to influence. If I'm writing an opinion piece, one of my goals certainly will be to influence; if I'm writing a how-to article, one of my purposes surely will be to instruct.

After deciding on my purpose, I begin thinking about who I'm writing for. Knowing my audience requires me to have a specific market in mind for my article before I begin it. Am I writing for women? children? senior citizens? singles? parents? Are they college educated? Are they Evangelicals? Fundamentalists? Main-line? How much can I assume they know about my topic? Determining the answers to these questions will help me know what vocabulary level to use, how much spiritual content is appropriate, and how much background information I need to include for readers to understand the point of my article.

The better I know my readers, the easier it will be to decide what tone to use when communicating with them. The tone I adopt also will be influenced by the publication I plan to approach with my manuscript. Does the magazine seem to prefer a formal tone, marked by long sentences and long paragraphs? Or, is it written in a chatty style with an abundance of sentence fragments and short, breezy paragraphs? Should I write in first person? Or, does the editor favor third person? I tune into the tone by carefully reading at least two issues of the magazine and by scrutinizing its writer's guidelines (available by sending a request and a self-addressed, stamped envelope to the editor).

With my prewriting activities behind me, I'm ready to tackle the research. But first I take stock: I have my idea and my title; I know what I'm trying to accomplish, whom I'm trying to reach, and how I'm going to package my message. Now I need information. Lots of information.

Popping the Questions

I'm inquisitive. Curious. Give me a topic and I'll think of a dozen questions to ask about it. For me, the research step of the four-step process has always been my favorite because it's like going back to school for a crash course in a single subject. When I'm done, I'm a mini-expert—at least for a little while.

Research can be gathered from a variety of sources in a number of ways: personal experience, observation, delving into library stacks, and conducting interviews. I usually combine two or three of these methods for every article I produce. Because interviewing is such an important part of free-lance writing, Chapter Six will offer tips on choosing sources and popping questions. Writing from personal experience and utilizing firsthand observation will be covered in Chapter Seven. That leaves library research—and that's where it all begins.

No matter what the topic is, I always launch my crash course at the library to see what everyone else has written about my subject. First, I check the magazine indexes for the most current information. If I find good material I make copies of it and put the copies into the file that contains my index card with my coverline scrawled on it. Next, I look for any books that might deal with my topic. I take notes from the books and store the notes in my file. Later, I'll add transcripts of any taped interviews I might conduct with people who are knowledgeable on my subject.

Case Study: Breast Cancer

If the first three steps sound confusing or difficult, let me convince you that they're not. Let me illustrate how they work by walking through, step by step, an article I once wrote for *Today's Christian Woman*.[9]

The topic was breast cancer, and the editor's request was open-ended. "We want to do something about breast cancer for our May/June issue," she told me on the phone. "We're not sure of the angle, but we understand that a patient's attitude has a lot to do with how well and how quickly she recovers. We wonder if a strong faith and a positive outlook wouldn't be major assets for a woman facing surgery and rehabilitation."

I was on my own. The topic was enormous, and the editor had given me the freedom to choose a direction and to take off. My only limits were length (2,500 words) and deadline (six weeks from our phone conversation).

I saw several obstacles. I didn't want to write a depressing article, yet cancer is a frightening topic. I didn't want to give the story superficial treatment, yet I lacked a narrow focus. I didn't want to concentrate on the few women I knew who had experienced breast cancer, yet I didn't know how to make contact with victims around the country.

First things first: a title. I decided to call my article "Life After Breast Cancer" because it narrowed the time-frame of the story to the post-diagnosis period, and it assured readers that there *is* life after breast cancer. Without ignoring the gloomy statistics (one out of eleven women will develop the disease), I wanted to concentrate on new treatments, support groups, and surgical options that have increased the likelihood of a fulfilling life after cancer.

The purpose of my article clearly was to inspire women to believe that life doesn't end with a cancer diagnosis, and that a strong faith and positive outlook can help mobilize the body to heal faster. Secondary purposes were to inform readers of new breakthroughs in cancer research and to influence them to be medical consumers and always to get a second (and third) opinion.

Since I was working on assignment, I knew exactly who my audience was. The typical reader of *Today's Christian Woman* is female, under forty years old, married, and with children. A warm, conversational, woman-to-woman tone seemed to be right for the topic, the audience, and the publication. I planned to include a lot of anecdotes as a way of downplaying the clinical aspects of cancer and emphasizing the human side.

Research. Where do I start? At the library, of course. It took me only an hour in the stacks to put together a list of several organizations that offer help to cancer victims. I found cancer hotlines where newly diagnosed patients can talk with persons who experienced similar diagnoses years earlier; a group called Encore, sponsored nationally by the YWCA, that combines exercise classes and discussion sessions for mastectomy patients; the American Cancer Society's Reach for Recovery program that sends volunteers into the hospital to visit breast cancer patients and to share information about prostheses, reconstruction, radiation, and chemotherapy. I jotted down the phone numbers of these organizations so I could request more information and ask for phone interviews with women who have benefited from their services. Because of the personal nature of the story I agreed not to use the last names of the cancer patients I would quote.

I discovered a sisterhood exists among breast cancer victims. They want to help each other, and if that means answering questions from a magazine writer, well, fire away. One call led to another until my deadline forced me to halt my research. My file folder, which once contained only an index card and a title/coverline, now was a fat sheath of notes, pamphlets, brochures, and transcripts. I was ready to write.

The Write Approach

The writing step (Step Four) is always the same. It requires the file folder, a felt tip highlighter pen, and a block of time without interruptions. I prop the index card (with my coverline) in a place where I can see it, and I begin reading through the file, page by page. It's at this stage that I must decide which of my research material to include in the article and which to cut from consideration. I'm immersed in the topic by now, and all the data I've gathered seems wildly interesting and terribly important to me. But it isn't all pertinent, and my word limit dictates that I discard much of it. My criterion of what stays and what goes is the coverline on the index card. If the material relates to the coverline, I highlight it with my felt tip pen. It stays.

As I read through the stack of information, I make note of any material that might work well as a lead (introductory) paragraph. I also mark in the margin anything that could be used as the closing of the article. By the time I'm done with this read-through process, I may have five or six possible leads and an equal number of possible endings. I then choose the lead I like best (or the one that seems best suited to the article's purpose, audience, and tone), and I write it down. The ending is selected in the same way.

It's essential to know your ending before you begin. Otherwise, writing your story is a lot like going on a trip without having a final destination. You wander a lot. Or, it's like trying to score a bull's-eye without knowing your target. It's easy to miss your mark. Every word, every sentence, every paragraph should move your readers toward your targeted ending. You must know exactly what that ending is if you are to successfully guide your readers in the right direction.

You now have completed an informal outline of your writing project. You have selected a beginning and an ending, and have sifted through all the material and designated what will be included in the middle (the highlighted portions of your file). The next step is to arrange the highlighted material into some sort of order that flows logically from the introduction to point A, to point B, to point C, and so on, . . . to closure.

Never throw away any material. You may mentally separate the usable from the unusable, but you discard nothing. Why? Because at least two or three (or more) articles will spring from this same file.

A free-lance writer makes a lucrative living in one of two ways. Either by selling a few manuscripts to a few very large publications that pay very high rates, or by selling a great many manuscripts to a great many publications that pay very modest rates. In the Christian marketplace, the latter is usually true. After investing time (and sometimes money) in building a file, the writer needs to wring out as much revenue from the file as possible. To do this, one might need only another index card and a different color highlighter pen.

Here's how it works: After I've completed my story, I review my notes. I look for a second slant that would utilize some of the material I mentally discarded for the first article. Perhaps one of the persons I interviewed and only quoted once or twice can be isolated as the solo subject of a profile article. Chances are, I only used a small portion of the information that was give to me. Perhaps, in the case of the cancer story, one of the organizations I discovered while doing research is deserving of an in-depth article all its own. Maybe the group is celebrating an anniversary and is a likely subject for a calendar-related story; or maybe its founder successfully overcame her own battle with cancer twenty years ago (a wellness story?).

The process begins again. I devise another coverline, write it on another card, and pick up another, different colored, highlighter pen. I read through the file, this time highlighting any material that relates to the new coverline. My notes are beginning to look like a rainbow, but the color coding helps me keep the two articles separate. I choose an alternative lead and ending (remember, I had found at least five or six possibilities the first time I ran through this exercise), and I'm ready to write again.

Recycling material into several spin-off articles is called multiple marketing. It makes sense and is perfectly ethical. The writer needs only to take care of one legal detail. Is the second article produced from the file a totally different property or is it merely a slightly altered version of the first story? If a different slant has been taken, or if a new lead paragraph's been used, or if a different set of quotes from different sources has been furnished, then the work can be offered as a new, original manuscript. If, on the other hand, the author honestly feels this is merely a slightly changed version of the original, then the editor should be told and advised as to where the first version was published. This would make the material second rights rather than first rights.

Many editors of Christian magazines encourage writers to engage in multiple marketing, especially if the writers approach publications with circulations that don't overlap. And this often is the case. Subscribers to *Bread* (Church of the Nazarene) probably don't regularly read *On The Line* (Mennonite). Readers of *Light For Today* (Lutheran) may never be exposed to *Baptist Leader*.

These editors realize that good authors can't spend valuable time researching and writing articles for bargain rates. But if an author can sell several variations of the same manuscript, it can justify the investment of time. Some editors ask only that the writer wait a certain number of months before offering a spin-off property to the next market. This happens most often when the writer is trying to recycle a manuscript without making any changes. If the article has been reshaped enough to be sold as a new property, no waiting period is necessary.

Great Beginnings and . . .

Whether you are writing an article, a short story, a nonfiction book or a novel, the opening few paragraphs warrant every ounce of creativity you can muster. Most readers skim the introduction and decide whether or not to continue. In the same way that a television viewer taps the pad of her remote control and moves quickly from channel to channel, a reader fans from page to page, pausing long enough to sample, savor, or switch.

A lead has three jobs to do. *First,* the obvious. It must grab the reader's attention. *Second,* it should tell precisely what the piece of writing is about; and *third,* it should set the tone and pace of the story. Creativity is vital, but so is honesty. Starting off with a humorous anecdote is a great way to hook a reader's interest, but it's misleading if the article very quickly becomes academic and serious. A lead should always be consistent with the rest of the piece. A reader feels cheated if a lead promises him meat and delivers whipped cream, or vice-versa.

As a writer, you have several ways you can begin each manuscript you create. You need to be familiar with a variety of them, although you'll probably develop preferences for one or two. Try not to get into the rut of starting all your stories in a similar manner. Force yourself to experiment. Be versatile. Among the most usable are the summary, the quote, the direct address, the teaser, the question, and the anecdote leads. Let's look at examples of each.

The Summary Lead

The most basic of all, the summary lead is a way to get quickly to the point and give the reader an in-the-nutshell overview of the information you have to share. Often the summary is stretched over two paragraphs, and contains the five *W*s and the *H* (who, what, where, when, why, and how).

The summary lead was developed during the Civil War when, for the first time, big city newspapers sent reporters into the battlefield to cover the action. These journalists had to relay their stories back to the newspaper offices via telegraph. A problem surfaced when the enemy started snipping the telegraph lines during transmission. To make sure that their newspapers got the gist of the stories, the reporters learned to cram all the major facts into the lead paragraph. If the lines were cut, all was not lost.

Summary leads are not often used by magazine writers, but can be effective under some circumstances. I chose a summary lead when I wrote about what happened at the annual meeting of the General Assembly of the Church of God several summers ago. The story was published in *Vital Christianity*, the magazine of the Church of God. It started this way:

> In sessions described as harmonious—even "ho-hum"—by some delegates, the sixty-ninth General Assembly approved with little discussion massive leadership changes and passed with little dissension a record $9 million budget during the group's annual meeting, June 16-17.

The five *W*s and the *H* are all present. Who? The General Assembly. What? Approved changes, passed a budget. Why? Annual action. When? June 16-17. Where? At an annual meeting. How? With little discussion or dissention.

The Quote Lead

Quoting someone's words is a quick and easy way to catch a reader's attention. The secret of an effective quote lead is to make sure the quote is colorful and really says something that is shocking, witty, thoughtful, or important. Impact is increased if the quote is short and stands alone.

Here's how Dennis Hensley and I began Chapter Two of the Christian mystery novel, *The Gift:*

"Shouldn't we call the police?"

It was Peggy Chandlar who asked the question. She and Marge Benning, the receptionist, were seated in Dr. Anderson's office in the administrative wing of Detroit Metropolitan Hospital. It was noon of the day after Dr. Anderson had made his remarkable recovery and after the John Doe had died. Anderson was seated in the large leather chair behind his desk. He was wearing sunglasses even though the office drapes were pulled nearly all the way closed.[10]

The Direct Address

This kind of lead strikes up a dialogue with the reader. The word *you* is always included as a device to reach out and point the finger at the reader. The writer's goal is to strike a common note and cause the audience to relate to what is being written. For example:

You never thought it would happen to you, but it did. You hadn't snapped your seatbelt in place because it was to be such a short trip. Then you saw the van approach, clearly out of control. You heard the screech of the brakes, and the next thing you knew you were in the emergency room of Community Hospital.

The Teaser Lead

The teaser lead plays with the reader and is purposely confusing. This confusion causes the reader to continue deeper and deeper into the text to decipher the mystery. The danger with a teaser lead is in letting the confusion go on for too long. An explanation of the mystery needs to be provided quickly so the reader doesn't lose interest in the writer's game.

Here's an example from a round-up article I once

wrote about Christian couples who are professionally as well as personally associated. They live and work side-by-side. The story first was published in *Today's Christian Woman,* then an abbreviated version was reprinted in *The Christian Reader.*

> The statistics are impressive: eighty-two years of married life, twelve children, and a stack of academic degrees from a variety of colleges.[11]

At this point, the reader is thinking, What? How could any couple be married eighty-two years! And how could they accumulate a stack of degrees?

The answers to these questions are provided immediately.

> Yet among these ten are only five careers. Theirs are team marriages—his 'n her partnerships—where three may be a crowd because two's the company.

The Question Lead

Beginning an article or story with a question can be effective if the question really prods the reader's curiosity and challenges her or him to try and come up with an answer. This kind of lead generally fails if the question is too simplistic or can be answered with a yes or no response.

An article on public schools vs. church-sponsored schools might start this way:

> What's the number-one problem in public schools across the country today? No, it's not drugs, alcohol or the skyrocketing drop-out rate. According to a recent study, it's discipline. Or, the lack of it.

The Anecdote Lead

Every writer has a favorite way of getting into a piece of writing, and the anecdote is mine. An anecdote is a little pearl of a story (often only a couple of sentences) that illustrates what the article is all about. It sets the mood. Readers like anecdotes because they're usually colorful, often humorous, and sometimes dramatic.

When I wrote a profile about a young college student who was on the threshold of a promising career in gospel music, I started it with this anecdote:

> Two years ago, Anderson University newcomer Amy Ransom cried every night and counted every day until she could go home to Coshocton, Ohio. Her mother offered long distance pep talks, her sister kept those cards and letters coming, and her dad consoled her to hang in there, honey, Thanksgiving's not so far away.
>
> Somehow she made it.
>
> This year, homesickness was no problem, but the holidays were still carefully marked on her calendar. Thanksgiving was wedged between Des Moines and Phoenix, Christmas followed California, and 1987 was rung out and '88 sung in at the Omni in Atlanta. (Anderson Herald, Anderson, Ind. 24 Jan. 1988).

If the anecdote works well for a profile article, it is also appropriate for an issue-related story. When I tackled an assignment for *Vital Christianity* about the surge of ethnic church congregations in big city America, I led with this paragraph:

> When Jacob Kakish launched his Detroit ministry door-to-door nine years ago, his goal was an uncommon congregation. He found what he was looking for behind the tidy storefronts and lace curtains of his urban ethnic neighborhood. His group now numbers seventy-five; few have been in the United States longer than three years; most are former Roman Catholics, and all prefer Arabic to English. Nothing is routine—even Sunday morning worship begins at one in the afternoon.[12]

The Combination Lead

Some leads are difficult to label. This is especially true of the combinations. It's possible to create an anecdote that is a quote and a question as well. For instance, the lead I decided to use to begin my "Life After Breast Cancer" story:

"When I told you that I had once had breast cancer surgery, do you know what you did?" asked Wendy, softening her words with a bright smile.

I shrugged my shoulders no.

"You looked at my chest."

Embarrassed, I started to apologize but decided instead to meet her candor head-on. "Do you know what I was thinking when you told me about the surgery?" I asked. It was Wendy's turn to shake her head. "I was thinking that you couldn't possibly have had breast cancer because you look too young, too pretty, too . . . too healthy."[13]

. . . Smooth Endings

If an introduction is the most important part of a story, the ending is second in priority. The closing paragraph is what the reader carries away with her or him. It fails if it is too abrupt, too drawn out, or if it leaves questions begging for answers. Reader satisfaction is always the writer's goal.

A lot of writers, myself included, often look for their endings in their beginnings. This makes their articles come full circle and gives the reader a sense of returning to the place where she or he started. For instance, If I open a story with a quote, I might wrap up the story with a final few words from the same source. Or, if I begin an article with a short anecdote, I might return to the anecdote for closure.

In the lead of the breast cancer story, I introduced Wendy as a young woman who had undergone surgery.

For my ending, I returned to Wendy and gave a subtle update on her condition. These were my final paragraphs:

> Four-and-a-half years after her surgery, Wendy prefers to view the brush with breast cancer more as a blessing than a burden.
>
> "Life is beautiful now," she says. "I feel more creative because I notice more; I look at things in a different way. I'm aware of moments because I know they're all we have, and I want my moments to be very, very full."[14]

With those final words I not only answer the reader's question (I wonder what happened to Wendy?), but I underscore the message of the entire story: there *is* life after breast cancer.

Knowing when to end a story is an art. The temptation is to state—one more time—what you've already said three or four times earlier. Or, you may try to tack on a tidbit or two of information that you forgot to squeeze in someplace else.

Don't do it. You can avoid never-ending endings by choosing your closing paragraph before you begin. When you get to that predetermined destination, you have no other choice but to stop.

5
500 Words about 500-Word Sidebars

EDITORS LOVE sidebars because they perk up a page. Readers are drawn to them because they're non-threatening. Writers see them as convenient little pigeonholes to tuck in wonderful information that didn't quite blend with the mix of the main story.

A sidebar is a tidy, self-contained package—sometimes put in a box, often placed behind a gray screen—that relates to, but isn't part of, a parent article. It's a colorful offshoot that rounds out and adds dimension to a major story. Because sidebars usually are only about five hundred words long, they attract readers who may not want to commit themselves to the longer stories. A reader will sample a sidebar, and if she finds it palatable, will indulge in the main course.

How do you write sidebars? Here are some tips that will help you succeed.

Be creative. While a sidebar can take the predictable form of an abbreviated article, it also can take a more unorthodox form such as a checklist, a self-quiz (readers love to learn about themselves via quizzes), a case study, 1-2-3 instructions to build something, or a calendar of coming events.

Look for other "voices." You don't always have to write the sidebar yourself. If you want to present a different point of view, counter to the one contained in the main story, arrange to have someone else write it.

An example of how another voice can enrich a story resulted when I interviewed gospel singer Sandi Patti for a cover story for *The Christian Herald*.[15] The focus of the article was Sandi as a new mother (she had just delivered her first daughter, Anna), and how the change in family status affected her career. During our interview, Sandi mentioned that in the early weeks of her pregnancy, while she was still touring, she kept a journal. In her journal she wrote short letters to the baby she was carrying. She said it made her feel close to the child. I asked if she had kept the letters. Yes, she still had them, she assured me. I asked if she would share two or three with the readers of the magazine. She agreed. The "package" that was published worked well. My story, called "And Anna Makes Three," occupied two-and-a-third pages of the December 1984 issue; her sidebar, called "Letters To An Unborn Child," filled the other two-thirds of the page.

Be original. It's very important that the information in a sidebar is not just an extension or an echo of the material that is presented in the main story. If I quote a person in the main article, I never quote her or him in the sidebar.

Think big. What's better than one sidebar? Two. Or even three. My article "Life After Breast Cancer" had three sidebars. The first, "Helping Children Deal With A Family Member's Cancer," was written by Janet Britton, a high school teacher from Ohio. She offered her advice in steps that were numbered 1-2-3-4-5-6. The second, "A Husband's Diary About Breast Cancer," was written by John Sloan, an editor at Zondervan Books. He took a countdown approach, beginning with the seventh day before his wife's biopsy and continuing to the day of her surgery and to the noncancerous diagnosis. The third sidebar, which I wrote, was a glossary of medical terms to help a patient in her dialogue with her doctors.

Keep it separate. When presenting a sidebar to an editor, offer it as a separately typed article. Label it as a sidebar, give it its own title, slip it behind the main story and under its own paper clip.

Most articles have sidebar possibilities. Learn to look for them. Not only do they isolate and call attention to interesting aspects of a story, but they isolate and call attention to you as a writer. An editor who receives an article and one or two supporting sidebars from a writer knows that she's dealing with a professional—a writer with savvy, someone who understands the business, as well as the ministry, of writing.

Sidebar Possibilities

Possible Article	Possible Sidebar
Profile of a woman who taught Sunday school for fifty consecutive years	Comments from several of her students on her impact on them
Teen-age suicide	Quiz: How stressful is your family life-style?
How to cope with a blue Christmas	The ten warning signs of depression
Planning a children's Easter party	Foods to fix (recipes) Games to play (rules)
Vacations your family can afford	List of resorts and destinations that welcome kids

6

Sourcery and Popping the Questions

MANY well-written articles are rejected because of a lack of "nuts and bolts"—quotations and their sources, anecdotes, examples, statistics, facts. Without moving from the typewriter, anyone can write, "The sanctity of life is being lost in today's world." But it takes some research to write, "In 1982, the number of abortions in the U.S. increased by seven percent over the previous year" (Writer's Guidelines, Pathways Press).

There's no getting around it. If you hope to succeed as a writer, you must first succeed as a researcher. And research means interviews. None of us can write well for long if we pull only from our life's experiences. Eventually we run dry of experiences and face two options: Either we stop writing or attempt to recycle personal experiences into new packages. If we simply adds some embellishments here, fresh anecdotes there, and then hope the readers won't notice that it's the same message, we'll fail. They will notice it.

All of us are familiar with writers—particularly plentiful in the Christian marketplace—who seem to have "themes." This is a nice way of saying the authors have been overpublished, have become predictable, even repetitive. Each new book seems to be a reprise, or a chorus, of the last.

How can you prevent this from happening in your career? By knowing how to tap into other people's knowledge and experience. The boundaries on your writing are lifted, and the possibilities are endless. No longer are you limited to what you've done, where you've traveled, whom you've met, and what you've thought about. Now your resources are multiplied as you fold in the thoughts, travels, experiences, knowledge, and acquaintances of others.

The way a writer accesses the huge body of information available to her or him is via interviews. These interviews can be used in three ways:

1. Background. The interviewee's knowledge is used, but she or he is never quoted directly.

2. Multi-source. The interviewee's quotes are used but her contribution is just part of a great deal of information provided by many people.

3. Profile. The interviewee is the main focus. She or he is observed, quoted, and described.

An interview situation can be as casual as a few words exchanged on the telephone, or as structured as a prearranged, face-to-face taping session. Depending on the writing project, an author might contact a source in search of one good quote to round out an article (multi-source), or, in the case of a profile, he may shadow his subject for several days, watching, listening, quizzing her, picking her brain, and recording how she reacts to situations and interacts with people.

Interviews are a vital part of nearly every kind of writing. And that includes fiction. Carole Gift Page, author of twenty Christian books and 750 short stories, once researched a novel by treating herself and her husband to an Alaskan cruise. She wanted to set her story aboard a ship and needed to have an accurate sense of how an oceanliner and its personnel function. As she and her husband enjoyed their trip, she informally interviewed members of the crew, took tours behind the scenes, and scribbled pages of notes. Much of what she was told and what she observed never surfaced in her book, but her understanding of life on board gave the novel a certain authenticity. The scenario was correct; the details were accurate; the dialogue was plausible; and the plot, which was fictitious, of course, took on added believability because the backdrop was so credible.

Not everyone can schedule a cruise and write it off as research, but anyone can interview a travel agent about what to expect from such a trip. Logical questions might be, What kind of weather is likely? How about accommodations? What's the typical dinner menu? Who takes these kinds of cruises? men? women? singles? families? elderly people? the wealthy? What kinds of clothes are appropriate for a cruise? What are the correct titles of the ship's personnel? Such information will help the writer accurately draw his or her cast of characters and set them free in a realistic setting.

The contemporary novelist best known for this kind of intensive research is James Michener, now in his eighties, who still goes on location to the destinations of his novels. To prepare for *Alaska,* for instance, he lived in Sitka, Alaska, for two years. He absorbed the scenery, talked to residents, listened to their speech patterns, and read local history. Again, not many writers can afford this luxury, but that doesn't mean the books they create can't be set in exotic places or that their plots can't occur at interesting points in history. Interviewing someone who has lived in a particular area is the next best thing to experiencing the destination firsthand. And talking to an historian can help the historical novelist recreate the past in fascinating detail.

Whether the writer's speciality is fiction or nonfiction, the writer treats her or his readers to moments they might never be privy to otherwise. For example, as an interviewer for several Christian publications I have taken readers behind the scenes at the *700 Club,* let them sit in on my chat with Dr. Jim Dobson, had them with me when I enjoyed dessert and coffee in the rural

Tennessee setting where gospel songwriter Dottie Rambo creates her inspiring lyrics, and took them along when I went shopping for tropical fish with aquarium keeper (and singer) Amy Grant. It's my responsibility to report what it's like to be in these situations—using the senses of smell, touch, sight, hearing, and taste—so that my readers feel as if they've been there, too.

Often beginning writers think salable interviews are limited to articles about celebrities. They think that magazines are only interested in stories about well-known people and that they, as beginners, will never have access to such personalities.

They're wrong on both counts.

Some of the most in-demand interviews are with people unknown to most of us. Unknown to us, that is, until the writer makes the introductions via his or her story. These people are women and men from middle-class America, with whom readers can identify. They are successful Christians doing God's work in unique ways. They might be teachers, nurses, counselors, volunteers, day-care providers, or lay leaders in the church. They have stories to tell that haven't been heard before. They are inspiring because after being introduced to them and learning about their ministries, readers think, *Maybe I could do something like that, too.* By finding and writing such articles the author accomplishes two feats: an interesting, entertaining story is told and readers are prodded into action.

Interviews with unknown people often are more enlightening to readers and more satisfying to writers than interviews with famous "personalities." The challenge of talking with celebrities is this: How do you uncover information that hasn't been told and retold dozens of times? Sometimes it's impossible. For instance, early in my interviewing career I was given an assignment to talk with the Statler Brothers, the veteran quartet well known for their country and gospel music albums. I dutifully did research on the boys and jotted down several questions I intended to ask them. One of my favorites involved how they got their name. I noted in my "homework" that of the four Statler Brothers, only two were actually brothers, and none was named Statler. I was convinced that I'd dazzle them with an astute question about the origin of their stage name.

Because I wanted to be *really* prepared for the interview, I called the Statlers' office in Staunton, Virginia, and asked to speak with someone who could fill me in on some details. Once in touch with their publicist, I began the conversation this way:

"I know the Statlers have won a lot of awards—"

She broke in. "Three hundred," she said. "Six gold albums, one platinum, one double platinum, three Grammys, and five Truck Driver Country Music Awards."

"Wow," I answered in genuine awe. "They've obviously been together a long time."

"Twenty years," she replied. "They've spent 43,000 hours together, played to more than seven million fans, traveled one million miles, and used 150,000 gallons of gas to get around."

I was starting to feel sick inside. Publicist? This woman was more like the company statistician. She could have found work with the NFL. "I suppose they've been interviewed a lot," I asked.

"More than 15,000 times in two decades."

Now I was downright queasy. I wondered what I could possibly ask them that wouldn't bore them to death. "And they've probably been asked the same questions over and over?"

"Right. For instance, they've explained the origin of the Statler Brothers name more than 10,000 times. If you use that question, by the way, Harold will probably answer it. He's the one with the deep voice. He'll tell you the name was taken from a box of tissues in a hotel room. Then he'll laugh and say they could have just as easily been the Kleenex Brothers."

You get the picture.

Design a Gameplan

Whether your interviewee is a household name or

someone unknown to readers, your approach to the interview will be the same, and identical skills will be needed. The only variations may involve allocation of time. Rather than plunging right into the questions, you may wish to spend a few minutes establishing a rapport with the noncelebrity interviewee. Help her or him relax by chatting about something you might have in common such as children, a hobby, or mutual friends. Be informal and "visit" with the person until your intuition tells you that she or he is ready to get down to business. Before asking your first question, explain the rules under which you'll be operating. Reassure your interviewee. Make the arrangements clear. There's no obligation to answer a particular question: just say so and it won't be included. If the subject wants to give material "for background only," then the ground rules are that this must be said before the material is shared. "Not for print" and "off the record" must be advance arrangements. Otherwise, you'll assume that anything that is said during the course of the interview may be quoted in the article.

I'm a planner, and I believe that designing a game plan prior to an interview gives the writer a sense of organization and saves time as well. In Chapter Four I explained the four-step process I use to create Christian articles. First, I distill the idea to coverline size; second, I complete the prewriting activities (I decide on the purpose of my article, I designate the audience I want to reach with it, and I determine the tone that is most appropriate for the project); third, I gather my research; and, fourth, I write the story. Interviewing comes under Step Three, researching. But the people I choose to interview for the story will be determined by Steps One and Two.

Keeping in mind the people I'm writing for (audience) and the topic I plan to cover, I list several sources that I might contact for information. These will be people who have impact on the audience I've targeted. Often I don't have specific names at first, but I know the types (or titles) of people I want to talk with. For instance, I once counseled a writer from Ohio who was working on an article about the importance of tithing. The point she wanted to make in her story was this: With good money management even a one-income couple with two preschoolers can give ten percent to their church, build for the future, and still afford an annual vacation. We began plotting her course of action by first indulging in a little sourcery. Whom did she need to interview? What sources must she contact for insights? I helped her make a list of several people (not by name but by description) who would be excellent sources of information: a financial advisor, a banker, at least two young married couples who tithe, and a spokesperson for a church. (The latter might talk about the importance of supporting the church, the history of tithing, and estimate how many people follow the practice today.)

As a writer you always want to choose sources with clout. Also, you want to quote people who represent several parts of the country, both sexes, different ages, diverse backgrounds, and, sometimes, contrasting points of view. In the case of the tithing article, the financial advisor might be a partner in a large counseling agency in Chicago, the bank official might be a female vice-president based in Dallas, young couples might live on opposite coasts (one a blue-collar worker and his wife from Spokane, the other a schoolteacher and her spouse from Boston), and the church official might represent the Southern Baptist Convention in Nashville, Tennessee.

The best interviewees are people with titles that smack of authority (director of a program, chairperson of the board, president of an organization), and people with a great deal of experience or education in the area about which you're writing. If you plan to offer your article to the local newspaper, all sources can be from your city; if you're writing for a regional publication, the sources should live in the region you are writing for; if you hope to place your story in the national press, your sources have to be from across the country.

Where do you find these wonderfully quotable people?

Here are seven places:

1. College, university, and theology school rosters. Too often overlooked, college professors are experts in their fields and usually have doctoral degrees to prove it. They're constantly doing research, are up-to-date on the literature of their subjects, and they love to talk to people who share their interests. Also, academicians enjoy being quoted because recognition enhances their reputations among their peers.

2. Continuing education catalogs. These books are gold mines of potential sources. Most cities of any size have schools that offer not-for-credit classes in everything from estate planning to computers to cake decorating. The people who teach the courses are usually enthusiastic experts who communicate well on their topics.

3. Yellow Pages. Most libraries have on their shelves telephone books from major cities. This is a way you can be sure your sources represent different parts of the country.

4. Public relations representatives. Every hospital, medical center, industry, governmental agency, politician, church, and organization of importance employs a public relations staff to handle inquiries from writers. Their job is to disseminate information, set up interviews, and answer questions. P. R. people are writers' best friends.

5. Other authors. Whatever your topic, you'll probably find that somebody has written the definitive book on it. Track down the book, read it, contact the publisher, and ask to be put in touch with the author.

6. Spread the word. Whenever you're researching a subject, let people know what kind of expertise you're soliciting. Somebody generally knows somebody who is the next door neighbor of somebody who. . . .

7. Attend conventions. If you plan to write an article related to education, find out when and where your state teachers association is conducting its next mem-

bership meeting. If you're researching a medical piece, be aware of any professional seminars that might attract doctors from within your region. Why make numerous long-distance phone calls when you can have dozens of potential sources gathered in one room at one time?

Everyone you meet is a potential source. Keep a little black book of names, addresses, and phone numbers of possible contacts. Many sources will last a lifetime if you treat them well. Each interview you do should be followed with a brief thank-you note. When your article appears in print, a copy should be mailed to every person you quoted in the text. Such preferential treatment keeps the doors open in case you need to pass through them again at another time for another assignment.

Determining good sources is only the first step in devising an interview gameplan. Contacting the interviewees is the next move. At this point you should be aware of three "thou shalt never" rules.

- Never agree to submit your questions in advance.

- Never allow an interviewee to "approve" an article before it is mailed to an editor.

- Never pay for an interview.

The reason for these rules are that they will help you preserve the integrity and quality of your work. If you agree to let your interviewee read your questions in advance, the spontaneity of the interview is gone. She or he will respond with prepared answers that the person may have written and rewritten, practiced and memorized to the point of the answers being devoid of personality and warmth.

A similar risk occurs when you allow the interviewee to read and approve your article before you submit it for publication. If given the opportunity, the person often will change and rearrange her/his words and yours. She or he will insert comments that were meant to be said but weren't and delete quotes that were actually said but regretted. The result is an overprocessed, too-pat bit of fluff that you may not recognize as yours.

Unfortunately, whereas editors of secular magazines seldom allow interviewees to read material before it is published, many editors of Christian publications automatically send articles to interviewees for their review and approval. When this happens readers don't get an unbiased glimpse of the person, but rather a touched-up self-portrait.

Finally, it is unethical for an interviewer to pay a person for an interview. Look at it this way: If you paid a high price to talk with a person and then you told him that you didn't think his comments were worth the money, would the person embellish them to satisfy you? Would truth be sacrificed to make the story worthy of the fee? Most people are honored to be interviewed—especially for Christian publications—because the articles are generally positive and result in excellent feedback. Good stories are told, good people are recognized, and good information is circulated. If you are ever asked to pay for a person's time, politely explain that you are not authorized to do that, and look for another source.

There are two exceptions to these "thou shalt never" rules. If your article contains a lot of statistics, numbers, or phrases that are unfamiliar to you—foreign words, legal or medical terms—it's advisable to ask the person who supplied the information to check the manuscript for accuracy only. Or, you can arrange to read to her or him on the telephone any paragraphs in question. The second exception involves sharing payment with an interviewee for her or his story. If you are working with someone who has an interesting experience to tell but is not a writer, you can make an agreement that allows you to write the story, with both of you sharing the byline and the payment. This is not the same as paying for an interview.

When setting up any interview, it's essential for you, the writer, to assert yourself as the person in charge. Remember, the people you interview are often dynamic, aggressive types with high-powered titles and busy schedules. They're used to being in control and will seize command of an interview if you let them. Hold on. Explain who you are, what writing project you are working on, how she or he fits into your research, and the amount of time you will need. Don't gush about all of the person's achievements, but acknowledge her or his contribution to the topic. For instance, your introduction might begin this way:

"Hello, Rev. Brown. My name is Mary Smith and I'm a free-lance writer working on a story about inner-city youth ministries. I understand that your church has a program there in Cleveland that is so popular you've had to expand your facilities. I'd like to hear more about it, because this is exactly the kind of success story I want to include in my article. Would there be a time I could drop by your office (or call you) for a short interview? It won't take more than a half hour. . . ."

An interview should never drag beyond an hour. If more time is required, arrange for a follow-up visit. (It's always a good idea to end an interview with this request, "If I need to clarify anything or if I find I'm missing an important fact, may I call you?" Don't overstay your welcome. Even if the interview is going well, keep an eye on your watch, and when your time is up, make some kind of concluding remark ("I see we're running out of time, and I don't want to make you late for your next appointment"). If your interviewee assures you he's in no hurry, you can continue your questioning, paying attention to clues he might give when he begins to tire (yawning, fidgeting, clock-watching).

Where you conduct an interview will contribute greatly to the success or failure of the meeting. Public places such as restaurants are the worse choices, yet how often we writers suggest to interviewees, "Let's talk over lunch." Concentration diminishes when we are simultaneously eating, asking questions, responding to the waitress, diving for the check, nodding at friends, and being lulled by background music. A much better choice is the interviewee's home or office. Here your subject will be most at ease, and while he or she is answering your questions you can be scribbling notes on the person's body language and the room's decor. Especially when you're writing a profile story you can learn a lot about your subject from the colors chosen for the walls, the person's preference in art, and how he or she interacts with the pets, children, and spouse who wander in and out. Only a visit to a person's home may reveal that your subject adores antiques, collects political buttons, plays the piano, and is trying to stay fit by pedaling on the exercise bike over in the corner.

Some writers believe that for every minute of an interview the writer should spend ten minutes doing research. An overstatement? Maybe, but a sharp interviewer always enters a question-and-answer session well versed in the topic under discussion and armed with a lengthy list of questions arranged in the order to be asked. Author Cornelius Ryan once estimated that an interviewer who has done her or his homework knows in advance 60 percent of the answers to the questions to be asked.

And about those questions. . . .

Plan to lead off with a thoughtful comment that will show your understanding of the topic. Win her or him over by letting the person know that you've researched the subject and are anxious to learn more. Try to phrase your questions so they won't elicit abrupt yes/no answers. Instead, use such openers as: "How do you feel about. . . ." "What is your opinion of. . . ." "Describe for me. . . ." "How do you respond to people who say. . . ." "Tell me what it was like to. . . ."

Particularly if you are doing a profile of a person, you will benefit from whimsical open-ended questions that will allow you to know the more private side of your interviewee. These should be used toward the end of the interview, after you've built a rapport, and after the person you are interviewing is relaxed and trusts you. Here are some of my favorite open-ended questions:

1. What are your three favorite books?
2. What do you like and dislike most about yourself?
3. Who makes you laugh?
4. What makes you cry?

5. Describe for me your idea of a perfect day.

6. In the play "Our Town" the central character is allowed to go back to earth after her death to relive one day of her past. If you were given that option, what day would you choose to relive?

7. What do you know now that you wish you had known at age 18?

8. What do you envision yourself doing in five years?

9. Who are your heroes, living or dead?

10. What person has had the greatest influence on your success?

Much has been written about asking questions, but little has been said about listening to answers. Dr. Paul Rankin once did a study to determine how much time professional people spend communicating, and of that time, how much is devoted to the different types of communication. Here's what he found out: The average white-collar manager spends about 80 percent of her or his working time in communication activity. Some 45 percent of that time is spent listening, and the rest is divided among talking (30 percent), writing (16 percent), and reading (9 percent). For writers who do a lot of interviewing, the percentage of time devoted to listening should be much higher. Unfortunately, while all of us have experienced years of instruction on how to read, write, and speak, few of us have ever taken lessons in listening.

A good listener/interviewer sits about four feet away from the subject, faces the person squarely, leans forward slightly, arms and legs uncrossed and eyes on the interviewee. If a tape recorder is used (and I strongly recommend it), it should be placed on a table between the two rather than passed back and forth, and it should be the kind that does not require a hand-held microphone. An interviewer should always ask permission to use a recorder, and if the subject seems nervous about having personal comments recorded, the writer might explain that it will save time, boost accuracy, and will allow the interviewer to enjoy the visit without getting writer's cramp. It also should facilitate the listening process since she or he doesn't have to take notes, review a list of questions, and try to make eye contact with the subject all at the same time.

There are other advantages to taping interviews beyond those you may tell your interviewee. First, by playing back your session you'll be able to relive the interview and perhaps catch details you missed the first time because you were nervous. Second, if you're not able to write your story immediately, the tape will make the interview fresh again, and the sounds will help you remember the sights, smells, gestures, and other facets that fade with time. Third, you can critique your performance as an interviewer. Did you ask good questions? Did you miss an important follow-up? Did you step on the person's answer by asking another question before she or he was finished with the last one? Fourth, you'll have an accurate record of what your subject said in case an editor wants verification. Fifth, you'll have every shred of information that was conveyed during the interview. This will be helpful if you decide to recycle the material into another article for another publication.

What kind of product you create from your interview transcript will be determined by you and the editor. Some publications prefer a straight question-and-answer format (Q and A) in which you write a two- to three-paragraph introduction and then alternate between questions and answers without composing any transitions. Other magazines like more of a narrative approach with direct quotes plugged in every few paragraphs. In either case, you will want to be selective in the quotes that you use, making sure they convey real information and insights. You also may want to clarify the quotes by deleting repetitive phrases and correcting any grammatical errors. Of course you should never alter content or substitute words unless you first check with your interviewee.

Probably the most fascinating aspect of conducting interviews is that no matter how many you do, you never quite master the art. Too many variables enter into the experience —how well prepared you are, the mood of your subject, the comfort level of the room where the interview takes place, the time of day, the topic under discussion, the chemistry that exists between the interviewer and interviewee, interruptions, the order you ask your questions, how you look, if he or she has had a good day up to that point, if you have a headache, if you remind her of her favorite Aunt Clara who used to bake cookies for her, or if you remind him of the ex-boss who fired him on Christmas Eve.

Although part of your job as an interviewer is to make the experience painless—even enjoyable—for the interviewee, the meeting is not a social call, but a business assignment for you. Regardless of whether it is fun, difficult, a pleasure, or an ordeal, a salable product must emerge from it. The best way to assure such a result is with preplanning. Choose your sources carefully, arrange appointments, prepare a list of thoughtful questions, create a comfortable environment for the taped question-and-answer session, follow up with a note of thanks and, later, with a copy of the published article.

As I said at the beginning of this chapter, most types of writing—even fiction—require interviews. Anyone who hopes to succeed as a writer must be able to effectively extract information from sources by asking questions and listening to the answers. Many people will argue that the exception to this rule is personal experience articles. However, even those, so plentiful in the Christian marketplace, are enriched by the input of others, as you'll see in Chapter Seven.

Writing from Your Own Experience

THE sixty-four-year-old man sitting across from me was a would-be writer fighting an inflexible deadline. He was dying of AIDS, and according to his Milwaukee doctors, he had less than a year to live. He desperately wanted to write his story before the virus made the task impossible, but he knew he had to hurry. His weight already had dipped from 190 to 156 pounds, his stamina was gone, and he quietly joked that his wife of forty years now easily outlapped him during their daily swims and outdistanced him on their afternoon walks.

He had contracted the deadly disease from a contaminated transfusion of blood that had been given to him after heart surgery. A lawsuit had been filed, the blood provider had been found guilty of negligence, and the man had been awarded a multi-million-dollar settlement. But no amount of money could change the inevitable; the only difference was that now he would die a rich man.

The story he wanted to write wasn't full of anger and resentment, but rather emphasized faith. He was a committed Christian and at peace with his grim prognosis. His message was one of forgiveness for what had happened to him and joyous anticipation of what was ahead. As I listened to his story—I had been assigned to do a magazine article about him—I wondered if he would complete his book. He needed time to distance himself from the events, time to gather his thoughts and select which details to include, time to organize his story for ultimate impact. But time was the single luxury he lacked.

Does Everyone Have a Story?

On the surface, writing from personal experience seems to be the easiest kind of story to tell. It's your story, after all, so there is little need to run around in search of facts, there are few (if any) interviews to conduct, and all the emotion you need is stored safely in your memory awaiting your recall. Writing autobiographical material surely should be as easy as writing entries in a diary.

But it isn't. The truth is, writing from personal experience may be the most difficult type of writing to do. Why? For the same reasons that seem to make it easy. It's your story, so it's naturally fascinating to you. (Will others find it as gripping?) You lived the events so you have no need to seek other persons' opinions on how they unfolded. (Can you be objective and honest?) Because you remember every detail you'll have no trouble writing with great precision every colorful tidbit of information. (Will you be able to distinguish between important aspects of the story and trivia?)

I'm reminded of a good friend who is a no-nonsense newspaper reporter with an uncanny ability to recognize a good yarn, prune away the clutter, and expose the message with maximum impact. He once confided to me that his greatest regret was that he hadn't kept a journal of his early years of marriage.

"I could have written a dynamite best seller," Jack commiserated.

I must have looked perplexed because he quickly

explained the blockbuster that he hadn't pursued. "I married a German girl who had a terrible time learning English when she first moved to the States," he said with a laugh. "She used to get so confused and come up with the cutest ways of saying things. I should have jotted them down because now I can't remember half of them."

His normally sharp vision was clouded by love, and he perceived a book of his wife's witty sayings as the best seller that got away. His strong journalism instincts failed him when they were applied to his personal life. Witty wifely sayings, he forgot, fall into the same category as baby talk and home movies.

Does everyone have a story to tell? Most likely, yes. But not everyone recognizes which parts of his or her life are of interest to other people. Even if a person is able to identify the marketable content of his or her past, there is probably a lack of ability to tell that story in a way that will sell. Judgment, objectivity, ego, emotion, and relatives get in the way.

To help you determine if your personal experience has publishing potential, ask yourself the following five questions:

- Is my story unusual—but not bizarre?
- Can readers learn something from my story that will apply to their lives?
- Can I be objective in writing my story?
- Can I be sued?
- Does my story have an ending?

Let's take the questions one at a time. Is your story unusual or bizarre? It's a fine line between the two, but you need to be able to distinguish one from the other. Your story can't be too commonplace or it becomes ho-hum, and even a gripping tale loses its salability if it has been told before. Tom Lashnits, senior staff editor at *Reader's Digest,* in addressing writers has said, "Dramas repeat themselves. How many times do people want to read the 'Please help me, my husband has died and I can't land this plane alone!' story? Such stories can become clichés, and writers should avoid clichés like the plague." (Yes, Tom winked on that last line.)

A marketable story has to be unusual, yet it's possible for it to be too unusual. If it's unique—a one-of-a-kind sort of situation—few people will be able to identify with it. Once an editor from *Today's Christian Woman* asked me to read a manuscript that had earned a split decision from the magazine's editorial staff. About half of the editors liked it, the other half didn't. After reading it twice, I aligned myself with the negative half. It was a true story written by a woman who had endured tragedy after tragedy. She had a rare, incurable disease that doctors had seen so infrequently that they didn't know how to treat it; her mother was terminally ill; her child had died; and her husband had lost his job. Even her strong faith couldn't balance and bring about a positive tone to all the misery that was squeezed into the two-thousand-word article. It was downright depressing in its uniqueness. She would have done better to have isolated and focused on just one part of her burden.

Next question: Can readers learn something from your story? The editors of *Guideposts* offer this piece of advice—"It's not enough for a *Guideposts* story to be interesting and informative; it must also build to a definite point—a 'takeaway' message that the reader might adapt to her or his own life to help cope with life's problems. This message, however, must be presented subtly and naturally, not sermonically" (Writer's Guidelines, *Guideposts* magazine).

One way to assure that your story has takeaway value is to follow what I call an "inside-out approach." Begin your story with a personal-experience anecdote, then expand the scope of the article to include information from other sources. For instance, I once approached an editor with an idea for a story about role reversal. After receiving my query letter the editor was interested enough to call me for more information. Exactly how would I handle the topic? The truth was, I wasn't sure. I only knew that my mother and I had experienced an interesting flip-flop in roles several years after she had become a widow. She was being "courted" by a widower whom she had known in her youth, and they had marriage on their minds. I was suddenly playing "mom," doling out advice, and fretting about this gentleman's intentions. She was acting girlish in spite of her seventy-plus years.

The editor gave me her approval, a deadline, and a word count: no more than 2,500, she cautioned. I felt the euphoria that every writer experiences after landing a firm assignment. But it didn't last for long. When I sat down at my word processor to begin the project, I was struck with a very uncomfortable thought: Did anyone really want to read 2,500 words (ten typewritten pages) about my mother and me? It was a cute little story, but it wasn't unusual; we hadn't come up with a wonderful solution to the role reversal problem; and we hadn't experienced any drama. I began to worry. How could I salvage this "great" idea that I had successfully sold to the editor of a very large Christian magazine?

I decided to use the "inside-out approach." I began with the true anecdote of my mother's courtship and my reaction to it. As quickly as possible I broadened the article to include insights on role reversal from several interesting and knowledgeable people. My working title was "It's Ten O'Clock; Do You Know Where *Your* Mother Is?" The opening paragraphs read this way:

The call was expected, but the news was a shock.
"You're what?" I asked, gasping.
She repeated her bombshell, slower this time, delivering it almost in telegram style so I could absorb every detail. Jack had asked her to marry him (pause), she had said yes (pause), they had set a date (pause), there would be a few friends and close family present (pause), and could I come to the wedding, please? (Long pause.) She added that she had splurged on a white silk suit from the Dynasty Collection, although at age seventy she didn't suppose she looked much like Joan Collins. Jack didn't think so either. He said she was prettier than Joan.

"But, mom, it's so sudden," I sputtered, still stalled by the initial bombshell. "You've only known him for. . . ."

"Thirty-five years," she filled in my blank.

"What's the hurry?"

"He's seventy-seven."

I should have heard it coming. Mom had flown to Massachusetts in December to spend the holidays with my sister. The two-week visit had stretched into two months after her friendship with Jack had been rekindled. For the past several Sundays when she called me long distance I detected a girlish giggle in her voice. At first I teased her about her courtship and privately dismissed it as "cute." Now I wasn't so sure. Mom was about to sell her home in Indiana and move more than twelve-hundred miles away from her friends, her doctor, her church, her volunteer work, and me, her daughter. Our roles were strangely reversed. I was cautious, she was giddy; I was full of counsel, she was full of plans; I was talking economics, she was talking honeymoons. Mom simply wasn't acting her age.

"How did Grama react to the news?" I prodded, counting on my ninety-six-year-old grandmother to support me with some sage advice.

"She says Jack's a nice boy."[16]

* * *

At this point in my story I turned the emphasis inside-out, from personal experience to external sources. The transitional paragraphs read this way:

Sociologists call us the sandwich generation. We still have responsibility for children at home, yet we have a growing responsibility for our aging parents. We're the filling that holds the family unit together. And sometimes it's a sticky job. As our younger ones try to grow older faster, our older ones work to stay younger longer. Much has been written about the first, but very little about the second.

"We don't have a lot of guidelines yet," admits Joe Womack, director of the social work program at Anderson University. "For so long we've had this stereotype of what a grandmother's role was supposed to be. She was supposed to be home doling out milk and cookies to our kids. She was supposed to 'act her age.' To some of us that certainly didn't include going back to school, dating, marrying, or returning to the job market after retirement. But now we have some transition going on."

* * *

From that point on, I pulled in information and anecdotes from a variety of sources: a man who runs an Elderhostel program at Ball State University; a program director at a Michigan senior citizens camp; and the executive director of a Christian counseling clinic in Dallas. After I had looked at role reversal from their diverse points of view, I came back to my opening anecdote for the wrap-up to the article:

My mother was one of the lucky ones. She met her match and he whisked her away in a sporty white convertible. Mom always said if you have to go over the hill, do it with your top down. They're currently living happily ever after in Rumford, Rhode Island.

Their wedding was lovely, and Jack was right—mother is prettier than Joan Collins. My grandmother also was right. Jack's a nice boy. I recently called them to wish them a happy third anniversary and to say I hoped they'd celebrate dozens more. I got the answering machine. They were on a getaway weekend in the Poconos.

* * *

Next question: Can you be objective in writing your story?

Some of the best personal experience articles and books are the result of an author showing her or his vulnerability, admitting to shortcomings, and sharing the less-than-positive aspects of her or his personality and background. The temptation, however, is to ignore, gloss over, or make excuses for anything that doesn't reflect well on his or her character. I know of a Christian athlete who refused to mention in his autobiography that he had been married twice. The omission caused confusion among readers when the man spoke lovingly of his wife, to whom he had been married for ten years, and adoringly of his sons, both teen-agers. Because his ego would not let him admit he had failed in an important relationship, he risked losing credibility with his audience. Readers are far too intelligent to miss a discrepancy of such magnitude.

Objectivity not only involves knowing what material to include, but also recognizing what details to omit. A good story begins at the point at which the "action" is about to kick into high gear. Chronological order ("I was born on December 4, 1960, in Boston, Massachusetts, where my father was a drill press operator and my mother was a homemaker") rarely results in what we call a "page-turner." Yet it's so easy to look back on our lives and think that every second is important. We believe that to overlook any detail would be to shortchange the reader.

To help you determine which events to weave into your story and which to omit, first decide on your time frame. When is your story going to begin, how many hours or days will it cover, and when will it conclude? Make it as tight as possible. Start just as the "what happens" is about to happen, and end immediately after the resolution of the problem/event. Even within the time frame that you have set, you should not attempt to include every morsel of information.

Being objective (and honest) relates to the next question: Can you be sued for something that you include in your story? Or, what is more likely, are you invading anyone's privacy by telling your story?

If you incriminate someone, you must be prepared to present evidence to prove your allegations. As far as invading a person's privacy is concerned, you may be guilty of this offense if your story causes the person any real embarrassment, harm, loss of reputation, or loss of income. Three options are open to the writer who is concerned that her or his writing might result in legal problems. The first is to fictionalize the story and alter the characters and plot so drastically that it is no longer recognizable; second, it can be "factionalized" by preserving the validity of the story and merely obscuring the names and locations to protect the persons involved; and, third, she or he can consult an attorney about the liability of the story as it originally was written. Perhaps there is no cause for concern after all.

Possible lawsuits usually aren't a major worry in the Christian market where exposés and investigative reports are rare. More common is the risk of causing ill feelings among friends and relatives who don't like their lives being publically scrutinized. I learned this the hard way. I once wrote an article about workaholism and used myself as an example. I included anecdotes about my husband and children and how my work addiction affected them adversely. I was surprised after the article was published to note that they were very uncomfortable with my "confession." They were used to reading mom's words in print, but not on a topic so close to home.

Finally, does your story have an ending? Has the conflict that you're relating been resolved? If not, you probably should wait until more time has passed before writing it. I'm reminded of a woman who experienced a devastating divorce. She wanted to write about it, but was having no success putting her thoughts on paper. She enrolled in my creative writing class to learn what she was doing wrong. We talked, and it quickly became evident that she simply wasn't ready to write her story. Her feelings were still jumbled. She was angry, hurt, and resentful. Part of her wanted to lash out at her former husband who had deserted her; yet part of her still hoped for a reconciliation. She hated him, and she loved him. She wanted him back, and she never wanted to see him again.

A reader looks to a writer for guidance on how she or he should feel about the people in the writer's story. In the case of the divorce story, the reader couldn't possibly know whether to like or dislike the ex-husband if the writer was uncertain herself. No satisfying ending can be provided for the reader if the writer isn't satisfied that the ending has occurred.

Probably the best advice to the writer who isn't ready to write his or her story is this: Keep a journal. I know of an author who began a journal the day her doctor told her something was wrong with the baby she was carrying. She poured her feelings onto the pages of her journal as she went through the traumatic pregnancy, gave birth to her seriously handicapped daughter, and endured the infant's death a few days after delivery. Much later, after she had come to grips with her loss, she wrote a beautiful story about the experience. Its power would give great comfort to other couples in similar situations.

Unlike a diary, a journal doesn't have to be daily, and it doesn't have to be a record of what happened. More importantly, it should be a record of how you felt about what happened. It can be written or it can be recorded on tape. For instance, after Barbara Mandrell endured a head-on automobile collision that almost killed her and her two children in 1984, she realized that the experience might someday be the basis of a book. She wasn't ready to write such a book, but she wanted all the details to be intact when the time was right for the project. So, she asked one of her sisters and her husband to talk into cassette recorders and to recount from their vantage points the event, the long recuperation, and the comeback. This taping process, similar to conducting interviews with key people closely associated with a story, assured her of a comprehensive look at what happened. Barbara could provide personal insights on how her strength in God was fortified and how she emerged a different person from the experience, and her sister and husband could add thoughts on how they witnessed this change. The tapes lay ready whenever she was prepared to take on the project.

The Necessary Ingredients

To write salable personal experience stories, you need

five ingredients:
- A good story.
- A sharp memory to recall not just the facts, but your feelings about the facts.
- A tough skin to withstand criticism of readers and friends who might object to what you did or how you did it.
- Time to have come to grips with the situation and to have developed a point of view so that you can guide the reader.
- The ability to write "faction." (You'll have to recreate dialogue from memory; you'll need to compress time to delete empty periods; and you'll take poetic license in slightly adjusting events to optimize the points you want to make.)

Two notes of caution: First, don't feel you have to have suffered AIDS, the death of a child, or an auto collision before you have something worthy of a personal experience story. Often a simple thought or an observation can be the basis of a poignant piece of writing such as a meditation. Since a meditation (sometimes called a devotional) is a maximum of 300 words in length, a brief personal anecdote can serve as a contemporary illustration of a verse of scripture. The main point of the verse is the same as the main point of the illustration. Space won't permit you to dwell on the anecdote, so the most effective stories are short and simple. A prayer, based on the verse and the anecdote, ties all of elements of the meditation into a memorable little package.

Second, don't be afraid to experiment with new forms of personal experience stories. In the past, most such stories have been written in retrospect, after the fact, after whatever happened has happened. But a trend now is toward writing a story as it is unfolding. This is especially true of illness articles when a victim doesn't recreate his or her experience after it is over, but writes it as it is occurring. Usually this requires a series of stories, each segment of which relates a stage of the experience. Such an approach has been effective in third-person stories written by an author who attaches himself or herself to someone going through a traumatic event. The writer reports it as it happens. Readers become caught up in such a series, develop a bond with the patient, and anxiously await the outcome of the story. A wave of such articles has come out of the AIDS epidemic, and at least one series earned the writer a Pulitzer Prize.

All the how-to advice in the world cannot turn some people into writers of salable personal experience material. Yet their stories deserve to be told, and their stories often are best told from a first-person perspective. How can a nonwriter produce a personal experience article or book? The way this is accomplished is by utilizing the talents of a ghostwriter. Many authors augment the income they earn from writing their own stories by writing the personal experience stories of other people. This practice is especially common in the Christian marketplace where autobiographies are particularly popular. Such books can be initiated in two ways. The most common is for a publishing house to play matchmaker between a writer and a person with a story. The editor may recognize the potential of a book but may realize that the key figure in the book is not trained to write her or his story. The editor works with a pool of writers and knows the particular talents of each one. She or he chooses the writer best suited for the project and offers a contract. The writer will either be paid a flat fee to complete the book (half due when the contract is signed and half due upon delivery of an acceptable manuscript) or he or she will earn a percentage of the royalties.

A second way such a book is generated is by a collaborative agreement between the person with the story and the writer. They jointly create a book proposal and submit it to a publishing house. The editor then must make two decisions: first, does she or he like the story, and second, can this writer (previously unknown) produce a salable manuscript. If the answer is yes to both questions, a contract is issued.

Good ghostwriters are highly valued by publishing houses. They have the ability to conduct exhaustive interviews with the persons whose stories they will tell, then go home to their typewriters and "become" those persons long enough to create their stories. When the book is published it carries only one byline. No credit is given to the ghostwriter for creating the manuscript. Nevertheless, knowledge of which ghostwriter wrote whose book is common within the publishing industry. If a project turns out well, a plethora of offers generally follow.

A variety of communication skills assures a writer of as much work as she or he can handle, and give the freedom to choose the assignments that he or she finds most appealing. This kind of versatility allows the Christian writer to shift from articles to devotionals to personal experience to poetry to song lyrics. "Bread and butter" jobs such as ghostwriting often pay the bills so an author can pursue her or his real dream—that of writing fiction—which is the topic of Chapter Eight.

8
The Truth About Fiction

AUTHOR Dan Ross was about to be included in the *Guinness Book of Records* as the world's most prolific living novelist (replacing Isaac Asimov) when the Guinness editors decided to drop that gee-whiz category. Too bad, because Ross's story surely would have been an inspiration to all struggling writers of fiction. Ross's first novel didn't appear until he was 49 years old—he's now in his 70s—and at last count, more than 325 of his titles have been published. Even more encouraging is his practically nonexistent rate of rejection: Only one book has been turned down in his long, successful career as a novelist.

But don't hurry to the library expecting to find a cache of Dan Ross titles. Look, instead, for Jane Rossiter, Tex Steel, and Clarissa Ross, which are three of his fourteen pen names. Ross's books are mass-market paperbacks, and he chooses bylines that seem appropriate to whatever genre of fiction he's writing.[17] The same name that works well for inspirational romances may not be right for an action-packed western. And neither name may gel with the mood of his teen-age nurse series.

If Dan Ross's success story seems to validate the popularity and marketability of fiction, it makes two additional points. First, to succeed in the fiction field Ross has had to write an average of thirteen books a year; and, second, he's had to be versatile enough to switch from action to romance to historical to western to gothic novels. His productivity and versatility have paid off, although some times better than others. Over the years he's earned anywhere from $300 to $100,000 for a single book.

The truth about fiction is this: It's tough to sell, and, unlike Dan Ross, very few writers make livings solely from their short stories and novels. Proof of these unhappy facts is in the numbers. Of the thousands of new books published every year, only about ten percent are novels. (The majority of books published are textbooks at twenty-nine percent and religious books account for only five percent.) As for short stories, you need only to check the table of contents of most major magazines to assess the market. Many run no fiction, and of those that do, the ratio is about one short story to every dozen nonfiction articles.

It's small wonder that fiction writers often become discouraged. When I was senior editor of *The Saturday Evening Post* I periodically received short stories from a writer who glued together every third and fourth page of his manuscript. He was so convinced that his stories were rejected without being read that he devised this "glue plan" to prove his theory. He decided if the pages of his manuscript were returned to him still stuck together, his theory was confirmed. Imagine my frustration at having to steam apart a story before I could evaluate it. If he had used his time more creatively in valid market research he might have figured out why the *Post* didn't buy his fiction. We generally limited ourselves to two short stories per issue, and the bulk of those stories were reprints from our archives. In its early years the *Post* had a reputation for discovering new writers and giving them their first exposure to a national audience. In return, the young authors sold all rights to the magazine. What this means now is that the *Post* has in its files stories by Mary Roberts Rinehart, Kurt Vonnegut, Jack London, and other famous authors.

Periodically the best of these early efforts are exhumed, brought up to date with a new illustration, and repackaged in a current issue.

If my friend with the glue stick seems inventive, he is outdone by Crad Kilodney, a Canadian fiction writer who got so tired of being rejected that he set out to prove that editors don't know quality when they see it. Kilodney had entered and had been rejected in a literary contest three times when he decided to pull his prank. He found several obscure short stories written by such famous authors as O. Henry, William Faulkner, and Jack London. He distributed them to friends with the orders to retype them, give them new titles, change the bylines, and submit them to the contest. They did, and all of the stories were rejected. What this proved is questionable, but Kilodney finally saw his name in national print for having concocted the colorful scheme.[18]

The anecdotes about Dan Ross and Crad Kilodney illustrate the obstacles that a writer of fiction faces. Even being as productive and versatile as Ross doesn't guarantee success. Writing is subjective, and a very good short story may be rejected by one editor and accepted by another for reasons of personal taste. The best example of subjectivity may not be the humorous one involving Kilodney, but the tragic one involving John Toole, author of *Confederacy of Dunces*. Toole suffered such depression when he couldn't sell his manuscript that he committed suicide. His mother carried on the effort to attract a publisher, finally convinced the small Louisiana State University Press to issue the book, and *Confederacy of Dunces* not only earned praise from critics but was awarded the 1980 Pulitzer Prize for literature.

As difficult as secular fiction is to sell, Christian fiction is even more difficult. The reason is simple. There are far fewer outlets for Christian novels and short stories than for their secular counterparts. More bad news: Christian fiction is more difficult to write than secular fiction. The reasons for that truth are not so simple. When a writer attempts to deliver a Christian message she or he is tempted to contrive plots that aren't plausible, characters that are too virtuous, scenarios that are unrealistic, endings that are too pat, and moralistic themes that are too blatant. There is little takeaway value for readers who can't identify with the one-dimensional characters and the happily-ever-after conclusions. Such a reading experience satisfies only those readers who seek escape rather than answers from a book.

And Now the Good News

All this bleak information is not intended to discourage writers from producing fiction. To the contrary, it is meant to make writers more aware of the pitfalls so that they can avoid them. The reason Dan Ross has had only one rejection in his long and prolific career is that he only produces a book if he is under contract to do so. Smart authors follow his example and send outlines and sample chapters to editors rather than completed manuscripts. Based on this representation of the author's work, the editor either rejects the offering or extends a contract. (We'll talk more about book proposals in Chapter Nine.)

Smart authors also request the fiction guidelines from all magazines and publishing houses before sending samples of their work. If, for instance, you hope to sell a short story to *TQ*, the monthly youth magazine from Back to the Bible, you would benefit from this advice that is offered in *TQ*'s writer's guidelines:

> Most stories we buy will center on the lives and problems of 14- to 17-year-old characters. The problems involved should be common to teens (dating, family, alcohol and drugs, peer pressure, school, sex, talking about one's faith to nonbelievers, standing up for convictions, and the like) in which the resolution (or lack of it) is

true to our readers' experience.

In other words, no happily-ever-after endings, last-page spiritual conversions or pat answers to complex problems. We're interested in the everyday (though still profound) experiences of teen life. Stay away from sensationalism.

What could be more clear than that? If you have a story in mind that is a fantasy or is set in biblical times, you'd be wise to shop around for another publication because, based on its guidelines, *TQ* won't be interested.

The writer who is determined to crack the tough Christian fiction market should spend time reading and dissecting Christian fiction that already is in print. When Dennis Hensley and I wrote the series of three Christian novels under the pen name of Leslie Holden *(The Legacy of Lillian Parker, The Compton Connection, The Caribbean Conspiracy)*, we prepared free study guides to help writers analyze the books. We did this for all the aspiring but struggling novelists we've met in our writing workshops.

Here's what we suggest writers look for:

1. The quick start. The opening chapter of any novel should grab the reader's attention and thrust her or him into the thick of the action. The author can play catch-up later by filling in the gaps about the background and about the key players. The old rule that urges writers never to begin a book with someone's birth or with a blast from an alarm clock (signifying the beginning of a day and the beginning of the plot) should be followed.

2. The character development. The question is often asked about which comes first, the plot or the characters. I've tried it both ways and prefer the characters. Readers fall in love with characters, not with plots. It's not what happens that is of the greatest importance, but how these endearing characters react to what happens. A word of caution: Some characters become so lifelike that they dictate their own fate. Alex Haley, the author of *Roots*, admits to becoming so fond of two characters in his *A Different Kind of Christmas* that he couldn't bear to kill them. According to his original plot, the twosome were supposed to be caught as they tried to free slaves through the underground railroad. Haley, however, became so attached to the duo that he changed his mind and let them escape.

No matter how lovable characters are, they should only be allowed to populate a book if they have a purpose. I suggest that as an exercise an author should jot down every person in her or his book or story and then defend the presence of each individual. Ask, what "job" does the character do? If she or he vanished from the scene what void would be left? Could another character pick up his/her duties? Unless the writer is trying to write in the Russian tradition with a cast of thousands, the dispensable folks should be eliminated.

The danger in Christian fiction is concocting characters who are predictable and are either too good or too bad. These fictional people also have a habit of doing ridiculous flip-flops at the end. After struggling with his problem for 180 pages of a novel, the main character happens on a verse of scripture or is dealt a piece of pithy wisdom and becomes a new person. In reality, people change very slowly. Some psychologists believe that our personalities are formed by the time we reach six years old. How, then, can a character do an about-face and assume a new set of values in the brief time frame that is explored in 200 pages? More often than not, what seems to be a major change in a character is actually an emergence of a personality trait that was always there but had never before surfaced. Some event in the plot triggered it to come forth. Whatever that trait is, it must be consistent with the character as we know her or him. In the end, that person should be only slightly different from what he or she had been at the beginning. The satisfied reader is left with the hopeful feeling that the character is on the right track, and that the future appears bright.

3. *Widespread audience appeal.* Too often Christian fiction is blatantly geared to female readers. True, the

vast majority of novels are sold to women, but editors like the idea of reaching both sexes. One way to do this is by developing strong male characters. Of the five key characters in my novel *The Gift,* four are men. I also attempted to broaden the appeal of the book by varying the ages and backgrounds of these characters. Since readers like to see themselves in a book I included an aggressive young reporter, a middle-aged doctor, a powerful executive, and an elderly man who must work against the clock to finish an unusual project before he dies.

4. *The presence of humor.* Many writers of Christian fiction take themselves far too seriously. They fail to realize that in addition to inspiring and influencing readers they also have an obligation to entertain their audience. Humor is a valuable tool that, when put into the hands of a skillful writer, can elevate a good product to greatness. It can break the tension in a serious plot, give readers a reprieve from a "heavy" story line, develop the characters through witty dialogue, and keep readers alert by sparking a smile or even a belly laugh.

When planning a novel, a writer should make a conscious decision concerning whether or not she or he is going to use humor. If the choice is to employ it as a device, then it must be decided how and at what points humor is most appropriate. As the author builds a chapter-by-chapter framework of the plot, he or she should pencil in where humor can bolster the work and help her or him achieve the desired goals for the story.

5. *The Plausible environment.* Nothing grounds a story in reality more effectively than props that readers relate to. If the setting of a story is extremely realistic, readers are more likely to accept a plot that is somewhat improbable. For instance, the plot of *The Gift* deals with a man who has the ability to transfer time from one person to another. This unbelievable concept gains credibility through a backdrop that is very contemporary, and characters who express through dialogue the same skepticism that readers feel. Here's how I used timely props in one scene of *The Gift:*

Dr. Francis Anderson was not a fan of auto racing, but Peggy Chandlar had decided the Indy 500 would help him pass the time. For that reason she had called the local cable TV company, asked about ESPN, and arranged to meet a service representative at Apartment 3-C promptly at 11 A.M.

The mention of the Indianapolis 500, cable TV, and ESPN clearly creates an ordinary stage for the extraordinary events that follow. Another example of grounding an implausible plot in a believable background is the phenominally popular film *E.T.* The idea of an extraterrestrial being coming to live with a California family is incredible, of course, but because the setting and the characters are so real and so endearing, viewers buy into the plot and adore the strange little thing from outerspace.

Many plots of Christian novels contain inexplicable events that authors credit to divine intervention—the healing that shouldn't have happened, the "stranger" who solves a problem and is never heard from again, the vision that occurs to a key character and changes her or him forever. But will sophisticated readers of the 1990s accept such easy-out conclusions? Your chances of selling gee-whiz endings are greatly augmented if you've played out your plot in a contemporary, believable environment.

6. *The pacing of the story.* Another problem that is common in Christian fiction is a plodding pace that practically lulls the reader to sleep. Planning a novel is a lot like composing a symphony. Some parts are soothing, some stirring, some light and playful, some heavy and somber. The most memorable of them are those that lead up to a climactic, emotional finish, cymbals and all.

The goal of pacing is to keep the reader totally immersed in the story until the cymbals kick in. To accomplish this goal successfully, the pacing should be worked out before the first sentence of the first chapter is written. By planning a book's pace the author can spot and avoid potential problems such as a long stretch of narration that bogs down the action and may cause the reader to skim a chapter or two.

In our series of books by Leslie Holden, Dennis Hensley and I found a pacing formula that was well suited to our plots and kept our readers turning pages. Chapter One was almost breathless in its pace; the key characters were introduced a half footstep before they stumbled into the predicament that would dominate the entire book. Readers were there, on the scene, to experience the fall and to become embroiled in the drama of the problem. In Chapter Two, the pace slowed in order for the characters to be fleshed out. Since a novel cannot succeed unless readers care about the characters and care about what happens to them, a bonding must occur early in the book. This bonding causes the readers to know and identify with the characters. Therefore, we generally spent most of the second chapter giving our main character a past, complete with family, feelings, and foibles.

By Chapter Five, we usually were ready to jolt our readers. We anticipated that they were beginning to settle into the comfortable flow of our novel, and we wanted them to be alert. So, we would drop in a subplot with different characters and a different setting. Often the main plot might have a woman as its protagonist, and the subplot might revolve around a male. From that point forward we "cut" from one scenario to another, taking care not to tire or confuse our readers by moving too fast. The two plot lines were braided together, each retaining its separateness, until they merged and blended at some point near the end of the book for that climactic finish that all readers love.

Christian Novelist in Training

Dissecting successful Christian fiction, collecting fiction guidelines, and studying the markets are just a few ways to better your chances of selling your Christian novel or short story. There are others.

- **Be practical.** The fate of Christian fiction is currently undecided. Many excellent publishing houses have been discouraged by weak sales. They point to their warehouses, bulging with mediocre inspirational novels, as proof of the public's waning appetite for stories with a Christian message. Several of these houses have pulled out of the fiction market altogether, while others have pulled back and are adding no new authors to their ranks. I know of one major house that made a last-ditch effort to salvage its fiction line by issuing a promotional brochure for its books and asking the books' authors to help pay for the brochure by accepting reduced royalties.

A writer can lessen the chance of rejection by avoiding publishers who are on record as not being interested in buying fiction. She or he should concentrate on those who accept fiction, study what they are publishing, then contact their acquisitions editors with proposals.

- **Diversify.** For many reasons—financial, psychological, and professional—writers should not limit themselves to fiction. They will sustain the sting of rejection more easily if they occasionally have success in another market. Even if they dream of writing a blockbuster that will equal *Two From Galilee,* they should spend part of their waking hours writing profiles, interviews, and salable columns. That's exactly what Marjorie Holmes did while her now-classic *Two From Galilee* was making its rounds (and being rejected) at every publishing house in the business.

By diversifying, a writer not only makes money but can fine tune her or his writing skills. Weaving quotes into a nonfiction article is very good training for persons who someday will create dialogue. Interviewing and observing people can be valuable for the writer who eventually will create characters. An added benefit of diversification is that editors will become familiar with a writer's work and may agree to consider the person's fiction for publication or at least may be willing to give the writer feedback on it.

- **Travel.** Fiction writers in training should never pass up an opportunity to see as many places as possible. They should take pictures and make notes about the destinations. These enriching experiences may someday be recalled as settings for their plots. I know a writer who jots down the names of restaurants, streets, landmarks, and other trivia so she can use the information to ground her stories in reality.
- **E-x-p-a-n-d your knowledge.** Since no one writes from a vacuum, authors must fill themselves with a variety of information that they can store, recycle, and work into their plots, scenarios, and characters. They should attend lectures, enroll in classes, watch public television, listen to tapes, and read constantly.
- **Mind your own business.** Anyone who hopes to make Christian fiction a career, had better keep up with the business side of it. The best way to track the trends is by reading professional publications such as *Folio* and *Publisher's Weekly*. Articles about Christian publishing are run frequently and give readers insights into who is buying what and why.
- **Know the shortcuts.** The smart fiction writer tests the marketability of her or his product carefully with a minimum investment of time and money. This requires the author to doff his or her creative hat in exchange for a salesperson's cap. A crash course in quick-change artistry follows in Chapter Nine.

9

Selling Yourself and Your Ideas

I LIKE A tough challenge. That's probably why I like selling inspirational articles to secular magazines such as *TV Guide* and *The Saturday Evening Post*.

That, and for three other reasons. First, general interest magazines—those available on the newsstand—have larger circulations. This means I can reach more people with my words. When I write for *The Christian Herald* I reach 150,000 readers; when I write for *The Saturday Evening Post* I reach four times that number. Second, I can touch readers who may not be exposed regularly to Christian material. Rather than reinforcing what readers already know, I'm creating an awareness of, perhaps even an appetite for, something different. Third, secular magazines have bigger budgets and can pay me more for my hard work. A two-thousand-word article in a Christian publication will sell for between $250 and $350; in a secular publication the same article will bring $500 to $750.

I also like to write crossover books. These are books with a Christian message that are acceptable to secular audiences. Crossover books aren't limited to the display racks of Christian bookstores but may be included in the inventory of any of the more than 21,000 bookstores located across the country. The most salable titles may even earn maximum exposure by being available in the highly trafficked B. Dalton Bookseller and Waldenbooks stores (combined, these chains have about 1,500 outlets). A crossover book and its author also may be candidates for guest shots on one of network television's talk shows. (An author's appearance on the *Today Show* is said to result in 3,000 additional books sold on that day.)

For all these reasons, crossover books and secular magazine articles reap similar, desirable benefits: They're a challenge; they reach large audiences; they touch unchurched readers; and they bring higher payments.

Let's talk about money. Writers have been mourning the shortage of it for years. Mark Twain suggested that we should "write without pay until somebody offers pay; if nobody offers within three years, sawing wood is what you were intended for." A. A. Milne had similar sentiments: "Almost anyone can be an author," he said, "but business is to collect money and fame from this state of being." And then there was Louis Untermeyer's no-nonsense advice to "write out of love; write out of instinct; write out of reason. But always write for money."

Don't be squeamish about expecting and accepting fair payment for your writing, even if you consider your work to be a ministry. Remember that Jesus said, "The laborer deserves his wages" (Luke 10:7); and we all know that writing can be very hard labor. No editor, publisher, proofreader, or typesetter in the secular or Christian field works for free—so why should a writer donate her or his efforts?

Much of the dilemma of what a writer should charge a publication is resolved by the publication itself. If you plan to write for magazines, you may never have to negotiate fees or quibble about expenses. Magazines have set rates, determined by the publishers and based on subscription and advertising revenue. Some publications pay by the word (ten cents per word is common), others pay by the published inch, a few have a standard honorarium, and some put a price tag on an article based on the amount of research and legwork needed to produce it. *Vital Christianity's* Richard Willowby, for instance, pays extra for a story that requires a writer to make phone calls, take a road trip, or sit in on a day-long meeting or program. Other publications allow an author to tally expenses and add the total to the invoice. (Usually a cap is placed on allowable expenses.) In an effort to build a dependable stable of free-lance writers, some magazines have created a fee scale that slides upward as a writer contributes more frequently.

As a way of making up for less-than-generous rates, some Christian publications extend perks to dependable writers. The editor puts the writer on the company's complimentary list to receive the magazine free; the writer's name is added to the publication's masthead as a "contributing editor"; the writer is sent copies of books that arrive at the magazine office in abundance from book publishing companies hoping for reviews; and the editor buys only first rights to the writer's work as encouragement for her or him to sell the material again.

Compensation for writing a book is more negotiable than the fees paid for articles, short stories, and poems. Book publishers have standard contracts, but a certain amount of stretch is built into them. The standard document may stipulate an advance against royalties of $2,000, the author may request $5,000, and the final agreement will specify $3,500 with half of the amount paid upon signing of the contract and half paid when the completed manuscript is submitted.

Most publisher-author agreements are steeped in legalese and will never make anyone's best seller list. Nevertheless, the smart writer reads and absorbs all the terms of the contract and takes notes on the parts he or she doesn't understand or wants to negotiate. In addition to the obvious money issues—advance money and royalty percentage of the book's retail price—items to consider include the following:

- Foreign rights
- Film, television, audio tape rights
- Reprint and excerpt rights

You'll also want to be aware of how often royalty payments will be made (some companies issue such checks annually, others do it semiannually); what kind of a discount you will receive if you want to buy a large number of copies of your book (a graduated discount rate generally goes into effect depending on the number you purchase); and what will happen when the book goes out of print (can you buy the remaining inventory at a greatly reduced rate?). You may want to add a clause that allows you, at your expense, to examine those portions of the publisher's account ledgers that pertain to your sales. Or, you may want to delete a clause that gives to the publisher first-refusal rights on your next book.

In secular publishing, many writers prefer to leave the contract negotiations to their agents. This isn't an option for most writers of Christian material. Yes, there are credible agents who handle inspirational and crossover books (for instance, a former executive director of the Evangelical Christian Publishers Association), but they aren't plentiful, and their fees (usually ten to twenty percent of advances and royalties) further diminish the Christian author's modest income. Besides, some publishers in the inspirational field still shy away from agents, preferring to deal directly with their authors.

If you choose to represent yourself in the marketplace, you'll need to polish your skills as a writer of strong query letters and professional book proposals. A query is used when you approach an editor with an idea for a nonfiction article; the proposal is your sales vehicle for either a nonfiction or fiction book. If you are trying to market poetry or short stories, you use neither a query nor a proposal, but send the completed manuscript. The reason for this is twofold: First, it's often difficult to describe the plot of a short story or the theme of a poem; and, second, so much of the value of a story or poem is determined by the writer's style, which can be judged only by a thorough reading of the work.

To Query or Not to Query

A query letter is nothing more than a sales letter that attempts to sell a magazine editor on an article idea. It also tries to convince the editor that the author of the query is the best writer to tackle the article idea. There are several advantages to sending a query rather than a completed manuscript for a nonfiction article. Among them are the following:

- A one-page query requires only two stamps (one for the query and one on the self-addressed, stamped envelope enclosed for the editor's reply).

- A query letter is evaluated by a bona fide editor; a complete manuscript is generally passed off to an outside "first reader."

- A query letter will generate a quick response, often within a week; whereas, a complete manuscript may languish on an editor's desk for a month or longer.

- A query letter can be produced quickly without research; a manuscript requires time and often money to complete.

- A well-written query is the sign of a professional author; novices generally send full manuscripts.

You can prepare your query letter at any one of three places in the four-step writing process. You remember from Chapter Four that I explained the steps in the following way: (1) distill your idea to coverline size; (2) complete the prewriting activities by determining your purpose, audience, and tone; (3) gather your research; and (4) write the article. A query may be sent to an editor either after you've narrowed your idea and completed the prewriting activities, after you've gathered your research, or after you've finished your article. The least desirable point is the latter—after you've written the article. Why go to all that work only to find out that the idea isn't salable? Or, why finish a two-thousand-word article only to have the editor inform you that the publication can use the idea but is limited to a thousand words? Or, why labor over one angle to the story and then have the editor say that a different slant is preferred?

The best time to write a query is after you've trimmed your idea to coverline size, decided on your purpose, audience, and tone, and have done preliminary research. This may involve going to the library and uncovering a couple of interesting facts or statistics related to your idea. The information will strengthen your query by grabbing the editor's interest and whetting her or his appetite for more. Still, you haven't invested hours in doing extensive reading or in interviewing sources. You won't feel resentful if the query fails on its mission.

Even before I approach an editor with my sales letter, I go through an exercise that lets me know if I can afford to do the article. This surprises some beginners who assume that of course writers always profit from their work. Unfortunately, this isn't true. But a writer easily can determine whether or not she or he will make money on a project. I do this by jotting down what I will be paid for my work and then tallying the number of hours I will spend in producing the article and the amount of expenses I will incur during the research step. I put a price tag on the story, then I decide if I want to pay the price and pursue the assignment by creating a query letter. I not only figure my time, long-distance telephone calls, and road trips, but also postage, library copy machine costs, tapes for my tape recorder, parking lot charges if I will leave my car at the airport, and film for my camera if I will take pictures to accompany my text.

I learned the wisdom of this exercise after a rather expensive experience involving a book assignment for a large Christian publishing house. I was paid a flat fee to ghostwrite a book for a man who lived in Dallas. Naturally, this meant I had to fly to Texas to spend several days interviewing my subject. My contract included no expense money, so out of my flat fee came a round-trip ticket to Dallas, a rented car, housing, food, and incidentals. My expenses eventually totaled more than a thousand dollars, which greatly reduced my profit on the assignment. Next time I negotiated a ghostwriting contract I made sure that the publisher picked up the travel tab.

How to Better the Odds

In writing a query letter I always put myself in the editor's shoes and try to think of every reason why she or he might reject my idea. Then I counter those reasons. It's been said that only one out of ten query letters results in a positive response, but by anticipating the editor's arguments I've been able to increase those discouraging numbers to seven out of ten.

Let's look at an example of a query letter I once sent to a very large, secular newspaper, *The Indianapolis Star.* The story I was attempting to sell was an interview with Sandi Patti. The problem was that Sandi had just launched her solo career and was virtually unknown to everyone outside of the gospel music field. I put myself in the editor's position and saw several reasons why he might not want to give me a favorable nod on the story. Assuming that he didn't know Sandi, he might question if Sandi were worthy of a major feature, or if she were one of those ardent gospel singers who was strong on faith and short on talent. Another reservation would involve Sandi's link to religion. Would the article be preachy and therefore be offensive to many of the publication's readers?

Anticipating the editor's fears, I wrote the following query:

Dear Mr. Cavinder:
When Sandi Patti was working her way through Anderson University recording Juicy Fruit jingles

in Indianapolis, her goals were to obtain a degree in music, a high school teaching job, and to marry AU classmate John Helvering. She admits she fell short; but two out of three isn't bad. The teaching job was put on indefinite hold last March when she was named 1981 female vocalist of the year and gospel artist of the year by the Gospel Music Association. This week she was nominated for a Grammy.

Her success is starting to show. First,—there's the two-story house in Anderson—the Helverings' only "splurge" so far. (It still doesn't have any furniture in the living room.) Then there's the modest office, a not-so-grand duplex on Grand Avenue, located within walking distance of the Anderson University campus.

Recently, Sandi and I spent a Saturday afternoon together talking about her career, her music, and her future. She was bright, candid, and witty.

With your permission I'd like to send you the article that resulted. On speculation, of course. Enclosed is a self-addressed, stamped envelope for your reply.

My credentials: bylines in *TV Guide, Saturday Evening Post,* and *Indianapolis Monthly.*
Sincerely,
Holly G. Miller

Although the letter is brief and light in tone, several strategies are worked into its content. In the opening paragraph I quickly establish Sandi's normalcy. Like many kids today, she had to put herself through school. She didn't wait for a miracle to provide her with the tuition money; instead, she traded on her talent and paid her own bills. The mention of Juicy Fruit gum adds humor, as does the sentence about the lack of furniture in the living room. Most readers (and editors) can identify with newlyweds starting married life on a shoestring. To counter the argument that she's just another enthusiastic vocalist who sings at church suppers and passes the plate to meet expenses, I end the paragraph with the bombshell: She's been nominated for a Grammy. The timeliness of the article is emphasized by the fact the nomination came this week.

Paragraph two accomplishes two goals. First, it lets the editor, Fred Cavinder, know that he will be among the first to "break" the story of Sandi Patti's growing success. The public hasn't been saturated with articles about her because her career is just beginning to explode. Second, the paragraph establishes a strong regional connection. Anderson, Indiana, is within the circulation area of *The Indianapolis Star*. Therefore, any mention of Anderson, the Anderson University campus, or a specific street name (Grand Avenue) intensifies reader identification. Interest is boosted by the knowledge that Sandi Patti is a "local girl."

Paragraph three merely lets the editor know that the basis of my article is a lengthy interview during which Sandi and I discussed a variety of topics. By mentioning the conversation I am giving the editor a choice of focus—I'm saying that I can produce an article about Sandi's career or about the gospel music industry in general. I reaffirm that she is an interesting person, witty rather than preachy, and candid in her comments.

The final paragraph establishes my credentials as the writer who can handle the story. I assure the editor that I am willing to work on speculation, which means that he has no obligation to buy the article after I have written it. I list three of my credits, taking care to include a local publication (*Indianapolis Monthly*) to let him know that I can comfortably write for a home audience. This paragraph is placed last because it is the least important. Many beginning free-lancers fret that their query letters won't be successful because they have no experience to tout. My reply is this: If you've written a good query, the editor knows you can write and doesn't need past bylines as assurances.

Many writers differ on what they believe should be the style and content of queries. They favor whatever has worked for them. For instance, some authors say that you should always specify how long your article will be. I don't agree. I'd rather leave the length up to the editor. I'm flexible and can write as many or as few words as the magazine can use. Some writers refuse to work on speculation because they fear a fickle editor may say yes to a query and then change her or his mind when the finished product arrives. Again, I don't agree. If an editor likes the idea that I have offered in my query, I know I can produce an article that he or she will want to buy. In all my years as a professional writer I have never had an editor approve a query and reject the article that followed (and that includes the Sandi Patti story).

A ploy that has always worked well for me is to create an opening paragraph for my query that can double as the opening paragraph of my article. If you look back at the Sandi Patti query you'll note that the beginning can do double duty. I like this approach because it gives the editor a sample of my writing style, it grabs his or her attention just as it will grab a reader's attention, and it saves time when I sit down to compose the article. The beginning is already complete. The style I choose to use in my opening paragraph depends completely on the writing style preferred by the publication that I am querying. I try to write in a way that will blend with the rest of the magazine.

Sometimes an editor will add a step between the query and the article. After she or he receives a query that is of interest, the writer will be asked to submit an outline of the suggested article. On the basis of the outline she or he will either agree to consider the finished article on speculation or give the writer a firm assignment for the article. The outline step may seem like extra work for the writer, but I find it helps me to produce a better article. By organizing my thoughts on paper, selecting the major points I want to make, and creating logical transitions from one point to the next, I've taken a giant step toward completing the article even before beginning the writing process.

For all the guidelines that tell you how to write a

query, there is an equal number of rules that tell you how you should not compose your sales letter. Specifically:

- Don't falsely flatter an editor by stating how much you love her or his magazine.
- Don't make excuses for yourself or apologize for your lack of experience.
- Don't use the salutation "Dear Editor" or "Dear Sir/Madam" (always know the correct name).
- Don't promise more than you can deliver.
- Don't send your query to either the editor in chief or the publisher (choose a lesser title such as managing editor).
- Don't simultaneously send queries for the same article to several editors at different publications.

An editor's positive response to a query is cause for celebration. But don't let the party go on too long. Magazine editors are a very mobile lot. They move from one publication to another, and an editor who has given you the thumb's-up sign on a query may not be in command when you get around to submitting your finished manuscript. The successor may feel no obligation to honor prior commitments.

How to Sell Your Book Idea

Approaching a book editor is more complex than approaching a magazine editor. The unfortunate truth is that only a small percentage of new trade books (written for the popular market) make any profit. Less than 5 percent of new titles sell 5,000 copies, which is generally considered to be the break-even point for the publisher. Because book publishing is highly speculative, acquisition editors require more than mere query letters to convince them to do business with a freelancer. They're interested in locating manuscripts and authors with long-term market potential. They want titles that can first be issued in hardcover and then be sold to a paperback house. They want books that will have broad appeal, will be steady sellers over a long period of time, will lend themselves to creative marketing, and will generate a following for the authors. Sometimes a publisher will take a chance on a new writer if the writer is likely to produce a number of books of increasing popularity over the years.

The decision to publish a book is serious enough that it is made by a committee of editorial staff members rather than by one editor. This committee, composed of key personnel from a variety of departments, makes its determination only after carefully studying the book proposal submitted by the author. Most proposals contain at least four elements. Let's look at each one of them.

1. Cover letter. More than a cordial note of greeting, this letter should state the topic of your book, identify its likely audience, tell what qualifies you to write on the subject, give its approximate length, and (particularly in the Christian field) explain the need that the book will fill. If the topic is not new, you should quickly establish how your book is different and what will make book buyers select yours over the competition's. Unlike the article query, this cover letter is not limited to one page.

2. Chapter-by-chapter outline. Write one to two paragraphs summarizing each chapter and explaining what action will take place in it. This multi-page outline will help the editorial committee determine your pacing and your ability to maintain reader interest throughout. Top off the synopsis with a table of contents.

3. Sample chapters. It's a good idea to send three, plus your introduction. The chapters don't have to be consecutive but should include your opening pages. Try to show your versatility in creating dialogue, scenes, and characters.

4. Clips of past published work. You'll be given more serious consideration if you are perceived to be a professional writer whose work has been recognized by other editors. If you have any clips that relate to the topic of your book, include them. Otherwise, choose your best.

Like a query, a book proposal gives a publisher an indication of what you can do. In addition to describing your product, it allows the editor to see what kind of quality standard you set for yourself. If your query or proposal is free of mechanical errors, your full manuscript most likely will be error free. If your sample chapters are well organized, carefully documented, and powerfully written, the balance of the book probably will exhibit these same characteristics. A query and a proposal serve as microcosms of the projects they promote. The editor will scrutinize the sales material to see what you plan to say and how quietly you can say it.

"Noise" is an important factor in the manuscript evaluation process. Chapter Ten will show you how to hold down the noise while writing with faith, hope, and clarity.

10

Cut the Noise

SHHHH.
Cut the noise.
Learn to be a quiet writer.

"Noise" is a communication term that means any interference that prevents a message from being clearly received. Noise distracts the receiver and breaks concentration. Like static, it blots out meaning, garbles intent, and can be downright annoying. Although we usually think of noise as something that interferes with our hearing, it also can mean anything that distracts us in our reading.

How does this apply to free-lance writing? Think of it this way: The editor is your receiver; you are the sender; and your manuscript is the message. What kinds of noise might prevent the editor from reading, understanding, and appreciating your message exactly as you intended it to be read, understood, and appreciated?

Unfortunately, there are dozens of possibilities, and many are out of your control. For instance, an editor may be tired, the phone might ring persistently, there may be worry about a presentation that must be made after lunch, a conversation in the hall could be just loud enough to disturb, or perhaps it's 11:55 A.M. and stomachs are growling.

Because such distractions are inevitable and beyond our control, we writers have to be able to quiet the types of interference that are within our jurisdiction. "Noise" that we have the power to squelch includes misspelled words, poor grammar, slang, redundancies, cliches, clumsy sentence structure, weak transitions, typographical errors, obscure vocabulary, mystifying jargon, overuse of capital letters, messy typing, single-spaced manuscripts, and hard-to-read type fonts. To an editor who is sensitive to the tiniest flaw on a written page, these are jarring noises that disturb just as surely as a sonic boom.

Too many writers are so concerned with the lofty content of their message that they ignore the nitty-gritty aspects of a "quiet" presentation. Faulty punctuation and other mechanical problems are viewed as pesky details that easily can be fixed by an editor. But what these writers fail to realize is that such pesky details often obscure their lofty message to the point of causing the editor to reject the manuscript. The noise drowns out the meaning.

Editors are meticulous guardians of the English language. Like master musicians who cringe at a single wrong note, they pick up on the slightest imperfection in content and delivery. While they applaud writers who experiment with innovative ideas and encourage authors who lead readers down new paths of thought, they insist that the innovation doesn't spill over to the mechanical side of writing.

Sometimes it takes years to convince editors to flex even slightly on one of their hard, fast grammatical rules. Perhaps the best illustration of editors' rigid attitude toward language comes in an annual survey that Richard Tobin, a Big Ten journalism professor emeritus, conducts among newspaper and magazine editors. The topic of Tobin's poll is how editors view the fine points of English language usage. As recently as 1982, nine out of ten of the editors replied that they found the split infinitive "abhorrent." In a tight vote last year the editors bowed to pop usage and finally agreed that there are worse sins than to occasionally split (oops) an infinitive. But they refused to budge on other rules. They vehemently turned thumb's down on allowing the word "chairperson" to creep into accepted usage. They still won't tolerate *like* as a conjunction ("She ate like she hadn't had a square meal in a month"). No one could convince them to permit the shortcut "and/or."[19]

Certainly a great manuscript is not going to be rejected because of a single misplaced comma or an overlooked and/or. But how many errors can surface in a manuscript before an editor becomes distracted to the point of losing interest and reaching for a stack of "thanks-but-no-thanks" notes? How many gaffes can be present before an editor questions a writer's professionalism and doubts the writer's ability to get the facts straight since he or she can't remember when and how to use semicolons?

Excellent writing can go a long way in hushing noise that is outside an author's control. Interesting text, flawlessly presented, can hold an editor's attention in spite of external distractions. That is exactly what happened several years ago when the manuscript for *The Total Woman* arrived at the editorial offices of the Fleming H. Revell Company. In Chapter One of this book I told you how the author—Marabel Morgan—found pockets of time to write the best seller, but I didn't tell you how her book happened to be accepted for publication. I once interviewed Richard Baltzell, the editor on the receiving end of Marabel's message, and he recalled for me the day he "discovered" *The Total Woman.* It was after lunch and he was anticipating another long afternoon of reading manuscripts. On a good day, he told me, he could leaf through ten submissions; on a bad day he was dozing after the first. On this particular afternoon he half-heartedly reached for a meticulously typed collection of bond called *The Total Woman* and waited for the heavy lunch to combine with the light text and set him nodding.

"At 4:30 I had read it all the way through," he said. "I knew I had something."

Quiet writing can have that kind of effect on an editor. (Marabel did not submit the scribbled and pasted pages on which she had created the book but rather, a crisp, professionally typed ms.) If it is fresh, seamless, flows easily, and is free of distracting errors, an editor can slip into its rhythm and be carried comfortably to completion. Such quiet writing is clear, logical, and isn't hampered by internal noise. In its best form it can even cut through external distractions and arrive at its destination intact.

Clarity of Content

One of the early decisions a quiet writer must make after choosing a topic is to select a form. In other words, does she or he want to package the message as an article, a short story, a novel, a nonfiction book, a poem, or a meditation? Which vehicle will deliver his or her message most effectively to its destination? The wrong choice can result in a noisy piece of writing. A short story that spans too long a time period, crams in too much action, and has characters who experience too much spiritual growth becomes implausible. Such a story would be better told in the more expansive, leisurely form of a book. On the other hand, a simple thought could have great impact as a short meditation, but loses its power when diluted by too many pages when it is stretched into an article.

The most common types of material and their word lengths are as follows:

Nonfiction article	1,200-3,000
Article sidebar	350-600
Short-short story	500-2,000
Short fiction	2,000-4,000
Adult book	40,000-100,000+
Children's book	500-2,000
Meditation	150-500
Poem	4-16 lines

The best way to determine which form is right for

your message is by making a detailed outline and deciding how intricate a story you have to tell. Begin with a clearly stated thesis sentence that capsulizes exactly what you want to say. It may be helpful to follow the advice of veteran columnist James J. Kilpatrick and think of yourself as a carpenter who is ready to build a house. Says Kilpatrick:

> The carpenter has to begin with a plan; the writer must begin with a thought. There must be at least the germ of an idea. Before the first board is nailed to the second board, or the first word connected to the second word, there has to be some clear notion of where we expect to be when we have finished nailing or writing.[20]

An outline is similar to a houseplan. Based on its sophistication, size, and detail, the writer will know whether the finished product should be a story or a novel if it is fiction; an article or a book if it is nonfiction. The final decision on length should be determined by content, not by the writer's desire to write in a specific form. As the editors of Reader's Digest point out, a manuscript should be only as long as it takes to tell a story. An outline will help you know how many words you need to use in order to tell your story well.

Don't make the mistake of thinking that outlines, like sentence diagramming, are something to be endured in high school English class and then forgotten. Most professional writers create outlines to keep them on track, prevent detours, and ensure clarity.

When Edgar Allan Poe wrote *The Raven* he didn't sit at his desk and wait for the muse to guide his hand in the creation of some mysterious masterpiece. He later likened his writing process to carefully solving, step by step, a tricky math problem. Before he wrote the now-famous opening stanza he determined that his result would be about 100 lines because that was a popular and marketable length. Then he selected his tone (melancholy), his theme (death), his refrain, meter, and rhythm. Even after all this he wasn't ready to compose his opening lines; first he completed the ending and, finally, turned his attention to the beginning.[21]

Clarity of Word

Knowing the right length, devising a logical outline, and determining what form your message should take will greatly enhance your clarity. But a quiet writer doesn't stop there. Just as she or he is concerned with the overall size and shape of the product, so is he or she careful about the writer's building materials—words.

"A writer lives in awe of words for they can be cruel or kind, and they can change their meanings right in front of you," said John Steinbeck. "They pick up flavors and odors like butter in a refrigerator."[22]

When Random House published the second edition of its dictionary in 1987 the book contained 50,000 new entries, most of which were words that have been integrated into our vocabulary since the first edition debuted in 1966. Our language is growing and evolving, and this means we writers have more choices available to us than ever before. There is no excuse for settling for a "pretty good word" when a little thought can guarantee the "perfect" word.

Words carry a lot of baggage. They can have gender overtones, positive or negative connotations, and geographic variables. The sender of a message (writer) can know precisely what she or he means when a word is selected, yet the receiver (reader) may infer a different meaning because she or he perceives the word slightly differently. To fully understand how words can take on subtle shades of meanings, try this exercise: Make a list of as many synonyms as you can for the word *clever*. There are dozens, and at first blush they seem very similar. But look again. Some imply physical cleverness (skillful, adroit, dexterous, deft,); some suggest mental cleverness (shrewd, witty, resourceful, ingenious); some are positive (intelligent, proficient); some are negative (calculating, cagey, cunning); some are female (coy, foxy); some are male (jack of all trades, handy). Yet they all mean "clever."

Some words have short lifespans. They come into vogue, are overused, sink to cliché status, then fade.

Writers have to be wary because such trendy words and phrases can cause their writing to become dated very quickly. Since 1976, a group that calls itself the Unicorn Hunters of Lake Superior State University has concocted a Dishonor List of Words Banished from the Queen's English. Members zap popular redundancies (secluded privacy, free gift, Easter Sunday), and wag fingers at newly invented words (womanizer, garageable, orientate), and takes issue with such nonsense descriptions as "living in poverty" (one appalled Unicorn explained, "I am not living in poverty; I am poor and living in Columbus").[23]

The quiet writer selects words with care and is able to defend the presence of each one. She or he agrees with Mark Twain's statement that the difference between the right word and the almost right word is the difference between lightning and the lightning bug. He holds out for the lightning.

Clarity of Presentation

The technical side of writing—the mechanical preparation of the manuscript—might be the most important contributor to quiet writing because it is responsible for the first impression. A cleanly typed manuscript isn't guaranteed a favorable verdict by an editor, but a poorly prepared ms. is plagued by "noise" from the moment of arrival at its destination.

The rules are simple and easy to understand if you remember that editors spend the majority of their workdays reading typed material. Guidelines for manuscript preparation take this into account. Each suggested rule is an attempt to preserve an editor's eyesight and sanity. Some of the rules are unbendable, others are more flexible. We'll look at both, beginning with the unbendable: paper, print, and postage.

• *The paper stock* you choose should be white and of standard size and weight. Never should it be lightweight (remember onionskin?) in order to trim postage costs, nor should it be the slick, heavy thermal paper that some copy machines require.

- Editors prefer *pica type* because it is slightly larger and easier to read. But most editors won't balk at elite type. Absolutely forbidden are speciality typefaces such as script, all-cap, orator (extra large, designed for broadcasters and public speakers), and others. If you use a word processor, be sure your printer is letter quality rather than dot matrix. Some editors will read dot matrix if you have a double-strike option (each letter is printed twice). Optical scanning devices (used increasingly in editorial offices to "read" typed mss. and store them electronically for typesetting) usually read each tiny dot as a separate character, making scanning impossible.
- *Always include postage* with your manuscript, query letter, and any other correspondence that passes between you and an editor. Lack of postage says you're either a novice who doesn't know the rules, you're overly confident that your manuscript will be accepted, or you actually believe that a stamp-less manuscript will gently nudge an editor toward acceptance rather than rejection of your work. Most Christian publications work on very tight budgets and can't afford to absorb the cost of return postage. The writer who neglects to pay his or her own way is perceived negatively. Such negative perception is also called noise.

Other, less emphatic, rules of manuscript preparation deal with the visual aspects of presentation and various modes of delivery.

An article or short story manuscript that arrives with a title sheet, or worse yet, in a plastic binder, smacks of a beginner. (A title sheet is fine for a book, but not for anything shorter.) Instead, center your working title about halfway down the first page, and type it in capital and lower case letters. There is no need to underline it, although many writers do this for emphasis. Drop down two lines and type your byline (this is where you indicate if you are using a pen name). Drop down an additional two lines and begin your text. The body of your manuscript should be double spaced, with each paragraph indented five to seven spaces and your margins an inch and a quarter all the way around. If your typewriter or printer has the capability of justifying the right margin (making each line the same length), don't use it. Editors prefer an unjustified (also called "ragged") right margin. Again, it's slightly easier on the eyes.

Your name, address, and daytime phone number should be in the upper left corner (single spaced). Approximate word count can be typed on the right side of page one, several lines down from the top. Some writers also include in that area the rights they are offering (first rights, usually), copyright information (©1990, Mary Smith), and Social Security number. None of this information is necessary since the author and the editor will negotiate rights after the manuscript is accepted; the work is automatically covered by copyright as soon as it is created; and the Social Security information will be requested and submitted after a sales agreement has been reached.

Every page after the first should be numbered at the top left, usually following the writer's last name and a slugline (a word or two identifying the manuscript). So, the second page of your article about the homeless might begin with this line: Smith/Homeless/2. This information is essential since editors like the pages of a manuscript to be secured under a paper clip rather than stapled together. Since the pages are loose, they need to be carefully identified in case they become shuffled.

If your submission is less than five pages, fold it in thirds and send in a standard business envelope. If it is five pages or more, mail it flat in a large envelope. In either case, include a self-addressed stamped envelope (SASE) for its return. Many writers also tuck under the paperclip a self-addressed postcard that the editor will drop in the mail as soon as he or she opens the envelope. This postcard merely assures the writer that the manuscript arrived safely at its destination and is in the process of being evaluated.

Technology is changing rapidly, and it is affecting the "noise" level of messages between editor and writer. Because word processing is now the rule rather than the exception in manuscript preparation, editors expect nearly flawless pages. The days of whiting out and typing over errors are gone. Whereas it used to be permissible to make minor corrections with a pencil, now such scribbles constitute "noise" and distract editors. Today's writers store their manuscripts on disks, and if an error is discovered during the proofreading process, a corrected version is printed within minutes. Innovations such as word processing programs that scan text for spelling errors also have decreased the noise in a manuscript, and, at the same time, decreased an editor's tolerance for such noise.

Methods of transmission are being upgraded. Floppy disks are being accepted by some magazines; fax machines and electronic mail allow writers to bypass the postal system in favor of faster telephone wires. While such technology may alter the speed of delivery, it doesn't affect the need for clarity of content, words, and presentation. In fact, it may underscore clarity because clarity helps communication move at breakneck speed. Modern editors are used to traveling at this kind of clip.

Don't get me wrong; editors are not heartless perfectionists. They're regular people who make their share of mistakes and tolerate (within reason) the errors of us writers. But they often work in publishing houses that are short on staff, time, and money. In the old days, editors such as Max Perkins could devote months to polishing a novel for publication. This isn't true anymore. Legend says that Thomas Wolfe's classic *Of Time and the River* arrived at Perkins' office in the Scribner's Building in three wooden crates and required two years to edit. The manuscript was hand written (Wolfe was 6'6" tall and had the habit of writing pages on top of his refrigerator and dropping them into the boxes unread and unedited). After the pages had been collated and the text deciphered, thousands of words had to be deleted before it was ready for market. No editor today has the luxury of concentrating on one project for so long.

Strive for clarity. Look for ways to cut the noise. Stand back and study your manuscript's size and shape; move close and examine its words and sentences. Give it the Aunt Betty test. (I once interviewed radio commentator Paul Harvey who told me that when he frets about one of his stories being too esoteric, or worse yet, boring, he thinks of his sister-in-law, Aunt Betty. "She's a wonderful person, an old-fashioned housewife," said Harvey. "She likes her information to slide down easily. If I think Betty won't understand something I wrote, or if it wouldn't catch her interest, or if it dwells on technicalities, I throw it away and start over.")

Finally, scrutinize your product's appearance and ask yourself these questions: Is it clean? Is it attractive? Is it quiet?

11
How to Get There from Here

THE OUTLOOK is sensational. If Christian publishing continues its present upward spiral, it will be a $5.2 billion industry by the year 2000.[24] And that's a conservative estimate.

More good news: About six hundred Christian publishing houses currently operate in the United States, some producing more than a hundred titles a year; Christian book sales are expected to tally an annual growth rate of from six to eight percent through the turn of the century; one new Christian bookstore opens its doors every day (somebody has to write the books and produce the magazine articles to fill all those empty shelves); and at least five Christian periodicals have circulations of more than a million subscribers (*Guideposts, Decision, Columbia, The Lutheran, Focus on the Family*). Such industry stats aren't surprising in light of a recent Gallup poll that confirms that the majority of Americans (54 percent) considers religion to be very important in their lives.

Interesting. But what's the point of all this data? Just this: By now you should be convinced that the time has never been better to launch a Christian writing career. This book has nudged you in that direction, and now it's up to you to continue the momentum.

Where do you go from here? What's next? If you finish reading this book on Monday night, what should you do about your writing career on Tuesday morning? What should be your next move as you work your way toward a recognized niche in the Christian publishing field?

Whenever I teach a writers workshop I caution participants to expect a letdown after they return home to their typewriters and word processors. Writing is a lonely business, according to the cliche, and the enthusiasm that students feel when they're a part of a buzzing roomful of writers goes flat when the number is reduced to one. The vision of success, so clear when shared over lunch or during coffee breaks, becomes soft. Encouragement and understanding are gone, and with them, the sense of direction.

Finishing a book can have the same effect. As long as a reader has another page to turn, she or he knows the mission. Where does he or she go next? To the next page, of course, or to the next chapter.

But now what?

At the conclusion of each of my writing workshops, I give participants a charge. I tick off dozens of "next steps" that they can take. The response the writers give to my list depends on several factors: the level of seriousness each writer has concerning a career in journalism; the amount of time allowed for writing; and whether the writer is a veteran or a beginner in the business of writing and selling thoughts. Let me do the same for you. Here are twenty "next steps" you can take after you read page 131 of this book.

1. *Become a clip artist.*

Prolific free-lancer Dennis Hensley is often asked how he was able to sell more than a thousand articles before he was thirty years old. Easy, says Dennis, who credits part of his success to the classified ad section of his Fort Wayne (Indiana) newspaper. He estimates that he finds twenty article ideas in each morning's edition. He also scours a small weekly paper for more story possibilities. "I circle any classified ad involving subjects that strike me as odd, humorous, unique, or upbeat," he explains. "Whatever comes to mind—a question to answer, a feature to write, a profile to develop—gets written down in longhand." Depending on his workload, he either follows through immediately with a phone call or he tucks his notes and the clipping in his idea file for later action.

Don't limit your clips to ads. Sometimes a statistic buried in a news article is just the detail you need to give weight to an opinion piece you're working on. (Example: An item printed in an education newsletter stated that in the past twenty-five years, delinquency rates among kids age ten to seventeen have increased by 130 percent. This statistic could add impact to an article about parenting or a story about a ministry that reaches out to teens.)

Often a humorous item can supply the lightness you need to balance a "heavy" topic. (Example: A filler in a daily newspaper estimated that a kiss of average intensity uses up nine calories, and some 389 kisses are required to lose a pound. Trivial? Sure it is, but it might be an effective eye-catcher if it were worked into a story's lead. Say the subject is love, and the writer begins with the kiss anecdote. She then admits that while the story is silly, it makes a valid point: that love can be good for a person's mental, physical, and spiritual health. She moves on to her more serious discussion.)

2. *Read your (junk) mail.*

Some of the best information you'll find comes not in the newspaper but in your bulk-rate mail. Examples:

> • A subscription offer from *Midwest Living* magazine boasts that the publication regularly features articles about "just plain folks" who have sincere values and a high regard for their neighbors. A smart writer translates this to mean that wholesome material about interesting people is in demand at *Midwest Living*. The only requirement is that the story has a regional link.

- A newsletter from a health maintenance organization devotes an entire page to dispelling myths about marijuana. This nuts-and-bolts information could someday be woven into an essay about drug use or could add authenticity to a contemporary novel geared to teens.
- A flier from the local Christian bookstore includes a copyrighted interview with Charles Swindoll. In the article, Swindoll discusses how and why he wrote *Living Above the Level of Mediocrity*, the book that generated a phenomenal 370,000 orders before it was published. Every writer could benefit from Swindoll's comments.

The point is this: A person doesn't doff her freelancer's cap when she snaps off her computer or slips her manuscript into the mail. A serious writer looks for story ideas, quotable sources, opportunities, facts, and anecdotes in all of her activities. Everything she comes into contact with has possible application in her writing life.

3. *Build a library.*

I collect reference books, and you should too. Countless trips to the library are avoided if you own up-to-date copies of an atlas, almanac, anthology of quotations, thesaurus, dictionary of foreign words, Bible commentaries and concordance, an encyclopedia of facts and dates, and industry listings such as *Writer's Market, Gebbie Press All-In-One Directory,* and the *Inspirational Writers' Market Guide.*

Forget the hard-cover coffee-table types of books. Your investment should be in inexpensive paperbacks that you can scribble in, crease the corners of, and turn open-side down on your desk. These books are to be used and replaced. Buy them through cut-rate mail-order houses, pick them out of the stacks on the bargain table at your local bookstore, or add them to your Christmas wish list. Always be on the lookout for timeless reference books that surface at library used-book sales. These might include history texts, grammar guides, and short story collections.

4. Subscribe to an informative service.

For this you'll need a telephone, a computer, a modem, and a telecommunications program. By making connection with a global information service you'll have access to reference materials that only the largest university libraries offer. What a tool for the writer based in a rural area!

Several information services are available (CompuServe, Genie, Dow Jones, Newsnet, and others), so shop around. The one I subscribe to allows me to monitor all the major newswires (Associated Press, Reuters, and others), lets me read electronic versions of newspapers such as the *Washington Post,* and gives me access to hundreds of specialized magazines and newsletters. I also can communicate with any of the 300,000 users of the service by sending messages via electronic mail.

The cost of subscribing to an information service is determined by connect time. If I am online for ten minutes, I am billed for ten minutes of connect time. All charges, of course, are tax deductible for the author who accesses information for use in his or her writing business.

5. Subscribe to a writer's magazine.

Everyone knows about *Writer's Digest* and *The Writer,* but are you aware of the *Christian Writers Newsletter* (a bimonthly published in Knoxville, Tennessee); *Living Streams: The Christian Writers' Journal* (based in Vincennes, Indiana); *Currents* (published by the Christian Writers League of America, with headquarters in Longview, Texas); or *The Christian Communicator* (a product of Joy Publishing, San Juan Capistrano, California)?

Sample the variety of writers' magazines that are available and select the one that fills your needs. Rotate titles and try a new publication every couple of years.

6. Attend a workshop.

Each spring, *Writer's Digest* and *The Writer* publish lists of writers workshops that will be conducted across the country that year. The most recent lists contained more than 400 entries. It's a buyer's market. Some workshops are specialized and geared to writers of mysteries, teen novels, travel, television scripts, poetry, and inspirational material. Some are fast-paced and cram several back-to-back lectures into one day. Others are more leisurely and are stretched over a week.

The best way to determine which seminar is right for you is to request the free brochures that describe the various workshops. Study the credentials of the speakers. Beware of famous-name authors who may spend more time signing autographs than teaching the craft of writing. Make sure that any university faculty members who are on the workshop staff are published authors with credits in the popular press, not just in academic journals.

A positive by-product of a writers workshop is the connections you make with editors-in-residence. Large publishing houses often send staff members to writers conferences just to scout new talent. For instance, one such roving staffer, Regina Hersey, an Atlanta-based assistant managing editor for *Reader's Digest,* goes on the road several times a year in search of article ideas. She explains to participants what the *Digest* is looking for, meets informally with aspiring authors, reviews manuscripts, and offers advice. Although her magazine receives volumes of unsolicited submissions (30,000 per month to the excerpts department alone!), she actively cultivates writers who show a flair for the kind of humor that the *Digest* covets.

"New writers are like new knitters," Regina says. "They don't want to start with pot holders, they want to make sweaters." At writers conferences she's able to convince them to think small and master one stitch at a time. She shows them how to prune single anecdotes to salable size.

7. Enter writing contests.

There are dozens of them. The best way to find out about writing contests is to check the various writers magazines (some of which, such as *Writer's Digest,* sponsor their own contests). Prize money varies, but the most lucrative Christian writing competition is the Amy Writing Awards, sponsored by The Amy Foundation of

Lansing, Michigan. A total of $34,000 in cash annually goes to the fifteen winners, with the first-place finisher taking home $10,000. Topics range from euthanasia to secular humanism to safe sex to the homeless.

8. Resolve to read a book a month.

William Faulkner once offered this bit of wisdom to beginning writers: "Read, read, read. Read everything—trash, classics, good and bad, and see how they do it. Just like a carpenter who works as an apprentice and studies the master. Read! You'll absorb it. Then write. If it is good, you'll find out. If it's not, throw it out the window."

Good advice.

9. Request guidelines.

Not only should you collect the writers guidelines of every publication you hope to write for, but you also should request the photo guidelines, the theme lists of upcoming issues, and the editorial calendars for the year. (For instance, *Light and Life* magazine annually publishes a pamphlet that outlines the emphasis of each future issue, explains the sidebars that will support the main stories, and gives deadlines for all articles.) Many editors are not willing to share such inside information since they worry that their competition will benefit from their creativity and duplicate their ideas. As you become a trusted contributor, however, an editor will invite you to look at the content she or he has planned for future issues and encourage you to "claim" the assignments you would most like to pursue.

10. Solicit book review assignments.

Consider these two facts: Most Christian publications contain book reviews; most Christian publications have very small staffs with little time to spend reading books. The problem that editors face is in finding qualified people to evaluate the latest in Christian literature. The solution that they've developed is to organize a pool of trusted free-lance contributors who can write tight and who love to read.

People like you.

The pay is modest but the rewards are great. Here are

the benefits you'll reap as a free-lance book reviewer:
- Honorarium (generally $25-100)
- You keep the book
- Your byline appears in a national magazine
- You're exposed to early publishing trends
- You get your foot in an editor's door

Most reviews are very short (around 250 words). They briefly tell what the book is about, discuss strengths and weaknesses, and make recommendations. Some magazines follow the policy that if you can't say something good, say nothing at all—in other words, the publications only review books that they recommend.

The best way to become a reviewer is to send your qualifications to the managing editor. Include a sample review that you've written in the style of the publication. Ask for an assignment and offer to work on speculation.

11. Join a writers club.

But be careful. Some writers clubs are little more than coffee klatches with members taking turns reading their work and heaping praise on each other. The best groups meet monthly, host guest speakers, take field trips to publishing houses, attend seminars, evaluate manuscripts, review books about writing, and sponsor public readings.

In addition to local organizations, there are state, regional, and national networks such as The National Writers Club of Aurora, Colorado. NWC offers its 5,000 members a manuscript criticism service, market reports, and access to dozens of free studies that cover the pros and cons of selfpublishing, literary agents, tax information, book contracts, and the like.

12. Go back to school.

Everyone else is doing it, so why not you? If you feel you need a brush-up course in English, check with the local community college or university to see what's available. A continuing education class in creative writing will cost less than a for-credit course, will be more informal, and won't involve grades and tests.

If the thought of reentering the classroom after a long absence frightens you, take heart in the statistics offered by the College Board: 45 percent of the students currently enrolled in college programs are "nontraditional" (older that twenty-five); and by the year 2000, the majority of college "kids" will be older adults.

One note of caution. Sometimes persons who claim they want to write will delay launching their careers by saying that they need to enroll in one more class, attend one more workshop, read one more book, sign up for one more correspondence course. Months or even years pass. At some point these procrastinators have to get down to the business of writing. Education should be ongoing, with writing done simultaneously.

13. Become a stringer.

Often called a correspondent, a newspaper stringer isn't a full-time member of the staff, doesn't earn a regular salary, isn't privy to the company benefits package, and rarely draws exciting assignments. Still, stringing for the local daily can open many doors for innovative free-lancers.

Here's how it works. Most newspapers don't have staffs large enough to send full-time reporters to cover routine meetings (city council, park board, school committee) that are conducted in the small towns that ring the city. But the editors want to include news from these areas, since the residents of the towns are subscribers. They solve the problem by hiring stringers who are willing to attend and write about the meetings. Payment is often determined by the number of inches published, with incentives added for stories that warrant page-one placement.

The money is less of a plus than the perks that accompany the part-time job. The writer learns and practices such valuable skills as interviewing sources, working under the pressure of deadlines, constructing interesting leads, weaving background data into current happenings, picking through an abundance of information and extracting the most important material. Try it. You will gain a professional affiliation. In query letters to magazines you can identify yourself as a writer for the *Daily Planet,* a fact that boosts your credibility and hence the chance for an assignment. Finally, you will come in contact with people you might not meet under other circumstances. These "just plain folks," with the sincere values that magazines such as *Midwest Living* are so fond of profiling, have a habit of serving on park boards and attending city council meetings.

14. Take notes.

Without realizing it, Park Place Church of God in my hometown distributes worship service programs perfectly designed for free-lance writers. Rather than the standard sheet of paper that has been folded in half with the morning's agenda printed on all four "pages," the program is folded in thirds with the last third left blank so worshipers can take notes on the morning sermon. If the minister makes a point particularly well, or if something said during the service sparks a thought in the writer's mind, she or he has a place to scribble comments for later study.

Ideas come at strange times and in odd places. A writer should always be prepared to record thoughts, questions, and connections when they occur. Writers' journals are very personal catchalls for these reactions. Unlike a diary that sometimes resembles a play-by-play account of a person's life, a journal is more a collection of a writer's feelings.

When Billy Graham wrote his best seller *Facing Death And The Life After,* he included material and ideas he had been collecting and chewing on for years. Some of his examples and anecdotes were pulled from personal experience, others came from outside sources. These were items that had had impact on him when he had lived them, read them, or heard a speaker mention them. Graham and his wife, Ruth, have a filing system for such treasures. They create a folder on a topic (in this case, death), and over a period of time they tuck in notes, thoughts, clips, and the like, that relate to the topic.

15. Expand your network.

In a speech to a writers group in Cleveland I once remarked that my knowledge of computer programming could be engraved on the top of a pin and there still would be room for the Gettysburg Address. After my talk, a young woman approached me, shook my hand, said she had enjoyed the program, and offered me her business card. It wasn't until I was back in my hotel room that I retrieved the card from my pocket and read her message: "If you ever need help, call me," she had scrawled above her name, Michelle Jones, and her title, computer programmer.

My son collects baseball cards; I collect business cards. He says his cards are worth hundreds of dollars; I wouldn't trade mine for a million. As a writer I'm only as good as my network of sources, contacts, associates, and friends.

Example: When I researched a travel article for a large secular magazine several years ago I decided that I wanted to talk with some hardcore travelers—military people. But I didn't know anyone in the service. I called a college classmate, now a civilian journalism instructor at the Defense Information School at Fort Benjamin Harrison. Although Patrick and I rarely see each other, we've traded notes and Christmas cards since we worked side by side on the campus daily.

"Who do you want to talk with?" he asked. "men? women? enlisted? officers? career military? big brass?" I felt as if I were placing an order: One sergeant, a female major, a colonel, and a colonel's wife, please, was my request. Within a few minutes he had supplied me with names, ranks, addresses, and phone numbers of everyone I needed.

16. Make a list of standing columns.

In an effort to reach out to readers and to give them a sense of participation and ownership in a publication, many editors have launched columns written by subscribers. Readers are invited to submit articles, and they are paid an honorarium if their manuscripts are selected for publication.

The best way to find out about these opportunities is

to check the table of contents of various magazines. Look for features with titles such as "Forum," "Viewpoint," "The Way I See It," "In Other Words." Read the column, taking note of its subject matter, its length, and its tone. Finally, look for any explanation of the feature that includes the rules of submission. For instance, at the end of the column "In My Opinion" published in *Virtue* are these words: "This column provides a forum for our readers to express their opinions about contemporary issues." This gives you guidance on the kind of content the editors are soliciting.

17. Change your habits.

Pulitzer-Prize winner Donald Murray offers this next step. His advice, included in his common sense book *Writing For Your Readers,* is to shake up your life just enough to see things from a slightly different point of view. Murray suggests, "Drive to work by a different route. Go to a familiar place at an hour when you're not usually there. Shop in a supermarket patronized by people on welfare. Stand in line at an unemployment office and listen to what people are saying. Sit in a waiting room at a hospital clinic."[25]

While you're doing all these things, take notes on what you see, what you hear, and what you feel.

18. Resolve to circulate queries and manuscripts.

Think for a minute: How many query letters, book proposals, sample chapters, short stories, and articles do you have in circulation right now? What good news might the mail carrier bring you today? What editors are you waiting to hear from?

At any given time you should have at least a half dozen projects in the works and in the mail. Resolve to release something for evaluation every week.

19. Acquire the tools of the trade.

You're going to need supplies. Not just paper, envelopes, and a pen to endorse your avalanche of checks—but real hardware (and, most likely, software). Create a picture of your concept of the perfect office. How is it equipped? Does it have a state-of-the-art computer, laser printer, file cabinets, a copier?

Now come back to earth. Compose a wish list and rank the acquisitions according to your genuine needs. If you plan to do a lot of interviews, you'll require a tape recorder; if you're mailing envelopes of varying weights, you might consider a postage scale; if you find yourself devoting too much time leafing through the dictionary to check your spelling, you may want to invest in a small electronic spellcheck and thesaurus device.

Brush up on the tax laws that stipulate what is deductible. Remember, you can't deduct more in equipment expenses than you made in your business. If you splurged on a $4,000 computer in the same year that you made $2,000 in your writing ministry, you can only deduct half of the purchase price.

20. Think of yourself as a business.

As in the case of any new business, you can expect to take a loss in the beginning. Your customer list will grow when word gets around the marketplace that you produce high-quality goods at a reasonable price and give excellent service (meet deadlines, correct problems, deliver the ms. with a smile).

As with any new business you should be willing to invest in upgrading your product. This might involve enrolling in a class, attending a workshop, hiring a typist, or buying an expensive reference book. Put yourself on a budget, and allocate a certain amount for "product improvement." If spent wisely, the money will bring a worthwhile return on your investment.

21. Learn how to be noticed

No, you're not done yet. One final "next step" needs to be taken. But it deserves a chapter of its own. If you are to earn more than pennies for your thoughts, you must learn the art of promoting your words. Chapter Twelve will show you how it's done.

12
P.S. On Promoting Self

ANYONE WHO has ever read one of Ann Kiemel Anderson's phenomenally popular books (*Hi! I'm Ann; Yes; I Gave God Time*) knows her fondness for the little *i*. Call it down style, lowercase or no caps. Whatever the label, Ann, in her more than ten best-selling books has never referred to herself as *I*, but always as *i*.

Her message comes through in her words as well as in the spelling of her words; Ann, the Christian author, is insignificant—a little *i*—in comparison to God, the Lord she writes about and the God she worships. A favorite theme in her books is the tug between doing God's will and fulfilling ann's wants (yes, she spells ann with a little *a*).

All Christians struggle with pride; but Christian writers have a special battle when it comes to publicizing their work. Somehow it doesn't seem right to promote the Christian message in our books and then to promote ourselves in the world and in the media. If reporters approach us and ask us to discuss our work, we humbly agree. Yet for us to take the initiative, contact the press, suggest a story for the Sunday edition (when circulation generally is the largest), or offer to be a guest on the local TV talk show to publicize our latest book, article or collection of verse—well, that's self-serving, egotistical, and prideful.

Or is it? Let's look at it from a different angle.

Leonard Felder, former director of research at Doubleday and now a writer himself, once offered this sharp observation: "Authors have to become more informed and talented at identifying and reaching readers through free or low-cost publicity," he said. Specifically, he urged writers to become familiar with marketing techniques several months before the release of their books. Why? "I give the credit for one well-written book selling while another well-written book bombs to the author's ability to spread the word about his or her book," he said.[26]

Nowhere is this more true than in the Christian marketplace where publishers don't have the generous publicity budgets that large secular houses have. They can't afford to buy print advertisements, design expensive bookstore displays, or underwrite a national author's tour to tout the release of a book, no matter how worthy its message. (Did you know that a full-page ad in a national magazine can cost $60,000 or more?)

If good reading material is to compete with trendy, pop books, then consumers must be made aware of its availability. That's where we come in. If we writers can get the word out via free publicity in newspaper stories or TV interviews, we not only have expanded our own ministry, but also that of our Christian publishing house. Our efforts allow the publisher's modest budget to be stretched and used in other ways to reach other customers.

Many inspirational publishing houses are starting to prearrange promotion for their authors. Servant Publications of Ann Arbor, Michigan, for example, sends an Author's Information and Promotion Form to every writer who signs a contract to produce a book. The six-page questionnaire asks for an autobiography, list of contacts within the media, names of acquaintances who own bookstores, suggestions of people who might endorse the book, author's travel plans and speaking engagements. The completed form is due at Servant headquarters six months before the book manuscript is due. This means that as the author is creating her or his book, the publishing house's promotion director simultaneously is creating a marketing plan.

Even beyond these publisher-driven publicity efforts, we writers need to spark some excitement of our own. We need to be more assertive. If we believe in our message we should try to amplify it in every way rather than shyly downplay our work and let our publisher worry about sales. If we succeed and our book sells well, we will touch more readers, change more lives, and we'll most likely be asked to write more books, which will touch more readers, change more lives, and on it goes.

How do you do it? That was the question put to me one summer during the Blue Ridge (North Carolina) Christian Writers' Conference. The young writer who asked it proudly displayed a small book of daily devotionals that had been published the year before by a West Coast publishing house. Some 7,000 copies had been printed, and twelve months later only 3,000 had been sold. The author was afraid that the sluggish sales might result in her book being discounted, banished to the back list, allowed to go out of print or, worse yet, shredded.

Her concerns were well founded. She had heard that 90 percent of a book's total sales usually are tallied in the first year, and that the "life" of a book is divided into four stages—introductory stage, growth stage, maturity, and decline stage. She balked at the last. It wasn't a matter of pride, she assured me. Rather, she believed in her book's message and had a collection of grateful letters from readers who said the devotionals had made a difference in their lives.

"So how do I do it?" she repeated. "Tell me how I can save my book, expand my ministry, please my publisher, and delight my family—all without leaving home or spending any money!"

She was joking, of course, but within a few minutes we had devised a simple list of promotional ideas that would require only a small investment of time and no outlay of cash to implement. Here was our plan:

- Visit the local Christian bookstore and ask the owners to consider an autograph party. Issue telephone invitations to friends, relatives, and local media to assure an enthusiastic turnout. Schedule it close to Christmas, Mother's Day, or some other traditional gift-giving occasion. Remember, an author is not asking for favors. Most bookstore owners welcome such events since they require little, if any, investment, and they increase traffic in the store.

- Generate a brief press release to be mailed to area newspapers. Announce that after a year in circulation the book of devotionals has brought positive response from readers across the country. Such a news release has maximum clout if it is typed on the publisher's letterhead stationery. Include an offer to do interviews. For out-of-state media, these interviews can be done via telephone.

- Check with your church library/media center about the possibility of setting up a special display of the book. Make sure an announcement of the display and the book is printed in the church newsletter. Every time book sales reach a new plateau such as 2,000 or 3,000, use the good news as an excuse for another blurb in the newsletter.

- Offer to speak at meetings of local clubs and service organizations. Don't charge anything for the program, but ask if a book table might be set up in case anyone wishes an autographed souvenir. Suggest that the group's presiding officer announce the books' availability and your willingness to personalize them. This casts you in the role of gracious guest rather than aggressive salesperson. Be sure that the local newspaper receives notice of where you will be speaking and what your topic will be.

- Send the book's publisher a list of newspapers and magazines that might be willing to review the book. Ask the publisher to furnish copies to the book editors. Personally deliver signed copies to book editors at newspapers in your hometown. If favorable reviews result, save them for use as endorsements on the jackets of future books.

- In your correspondence with your publisher, suggest that your book might be a good selection for one of the twenty-two religious book clubs that operate in the U.S. The largest is Family Bookshelf with some 84,000 members. Urge the publisher to send a proposal on your behalf.

- Call hosts of local TV talk shows and radio call-in broadcasts. Most programming directors are delighted to find interesting authors willing to make guest appearances. Be willing and interesting. Also, alert your publisher if you are invited to appear on any shows. He or she will want to contact bookstores in the area since viewers and listeners will be motivated to buy your book. Extra copies may be needed at the book outlets within the broadcast service area.

- Write to inspirational magazines and suggest that they publish excerpts from the book. Supply sharp black and white photographs in case the editors want to depict the author behind the words. Generally, publications use casual photos rather than formal portraits. Have a selection of both types available. Hope that you'll need them.

- Make a list of all your personal and professional affiliations: college alumni associations, honoraries, service clubs, fraternity, sorority, church affiliation, veterans group, community organizations. Do they have publications that are mailed to members? If so, send them an announcement of the book and explain that you, the author, belong to their group.

- Tell your publisher about any upcoming trips or vacations you're planning. While a publisher might not be willing to underwrite a publicity tour, often the publisher will arrange for media coverage if an author is on the road at her or his own expense.

- Use one aspect of your writing career to boost the others. Many magazines include a line or two at the end of an article to identity the author of the article. If you are still writing for magazines (and you should be), ask that the title of your book be mentioned in this author's recognition note (called a "bionote").

- Write to family and friends and ask them to contact their local bookstores and libraries and request the book. Create a coast-to-coast groundswell of interest. This is especially effective with book chains where sales are carefully tracked for signs of potential best sellers.

- Be aware of the important role that premium sales can play in your book's success. If you know of a regional or national ministry that might want to purchase large quantities of your book as giveaways to their donors and supporters, suggest that your publisher make contact with the group.

Before you implement this simple, no-cost publicity campaign, be sure to inform your publisher of exactly what you have planned. This will prevent overlap and duplication of efforts. Be aware that the most effective publicity is generated before the book's release. This creates excitement and anticipation. As tangible results of your campaign become apparent, supply your publisher with the "evidence." These clippings of newspaper and magazine articles, tapes of radio and TV interviews, and attendance figures from autograph parties prove that you are committed to the book and are willing to share the responsibility of promoting it. The author/publisher partnership is strengthened, and the likelihood of another joint venture is improved. Everyone wins: the reader, the author, and the publisher. Rather than promoting himself or herself—the little *i*—the writer has succeeded in spreading the Word.

And that's a capital idea.

Coming to Terms with Writing: a Glossary

ADVANCE. An advance against royalties is an amount of money paid to an author by a publisher before the author's book is published. Half of the advance usually is issued when the writer signs the contract, followed by the second half which is paid when the manuscript is submitted and accepted. The advance is deducted from profits (royalties) earned when the book goes on the market.

AGENT. Also called an author's representative, an agent is a marketing expert who knows the tastes, needs, budgets, and personnel at various publishing houses. She or he circulates an author's manuscripts, negotiates and closes contracts, monitors royalty payments, and gives feedback on book ideas and proposals. Agents work on a percentage of the earnings that they negotiate on the writer's behalf. This cut is usually ten-fifteen percent. The majority of authors of Christian material do not use agents, although industry forecasters expect this to change. Many Christian publishing houses prefer to negotiate directly with authors, and many agents feel the financial benefits of Christian publishing aren't lucrative enough to justify their efforts.

ARTICLE MEMO. An alternative to the query letter, the article memo begins with a proposed article's title, the lead paragraph, and a thesis sentence.

ASSIGNMENT. When an editor requests a specific article from a specific writer, the writer is working on assignment rather than on speculation. If the article is canceled for any reason, a kill fee should be paid to the writer.

ASSOCIATE EDITOR, ASSISTANT EDITOR, EDITORIAL ASSISTANT, CONTRIBUTING EDITOR. A pecking order, based on job responsibility and other factors, exists within every editorial staff. A writer should check the masthead of a publication to learn the hierarchy of the organization. This way she or he will know whom to query. Depending on the size of the staff, a magazine might have several senior editors, executive editors, and department editors. Generally, an associate editor works under the editor; an assistant editor is subordinate to an associate editor, and an editorial assistant is an entry-level position. Contributing editors are not on staff, but regularly publish in the magazine.

ATTRIBUTION. Unless the author is an expert on a particular topic, information gathering will come from outside sources. The author must be sure to identify the information used and credit (attribute) the sources. This is done either by direct quote ("Don't write about Man," said E. B. White. "Write about a man.") or by paraphrase (According to Voltaire, adjectives are enemies of nouns).

BIONOTE. Usually printed in small type at the end of an article or story, a bionote explains who the writer is. This is an excellent place to promote a current project: "Mary Smith is the author of the soon-to-be-released book published by Warner Press."

BRIGHTS. Short in length, a bright is a complete story or anecdote that entertains and lifts up readers. Editors often keep a reserve of brights on file to use as fillers. A writer can submit several at a time, but each should be typed on a separate sheet of paper.

CAPTIONS/CUTLINES. Whenever a free-lancer submits photos with a manuscript he or she should include a brief explanation of the pictures' contents. These words, called captions or cutlines, should offer new information other than what already is contained in the article.

CONTRIBUTOR'S COPIES. Publications that cannot afford to pay money to writers often offer contributor's copies in exchange for a manuscript. Beginning writers sometimes will agree to such an arrangement in order to establish themselves as published authors.

CO-PUBLISHING. When a writer and a publisher agree to split the costs and profits of publication, the joint project is called co-publishing.

COPY. Copy is the editorial term given to any typewritten material offered for publication. Clean copy means the submission is free of mechanical errors (spelling, typos, punctuation, grammatical problems).

© **COPYRIGHT.** Copyright protects unpublished and published works from unlawful use by persons other than the works' creators. No copyright registration is required, although there are some advantages to paying a fee and obtaining registration from the government. (The government receives more than 500,000 applications for registration each year.) Three circulars that relate to the copyright law are Circulars Rl (Copyright Basics), R2 (Publications on Copyright), and R99 (Highlights of the Current Copyright Law). All three are available free by writing to the Copyright Office, Library of Congress, Washington, DC 20559.

COVER LETTER. Not to be confused with a query, a cover letter accompanies a finished manuscript and usually briefly explains that "enclosed is a short, inspirational story geared to children ages — to —. Thank you for considering it for publication." Many free-lancers don't include cover letters because the information contained in them also is on page one of the manuscript (author's name, address, phone number).

COVERLINE. Magazines that depend on newsstand sales for a major chunk of their circulation (in addition to subscriptions) use coverlines to attract buyers. A coverline is a short phrase printed on the cover of a magazine to promote an article inside. Most magazines use at least four coverlines per issue. Editors always are looking for articles that are interesting, timely, and controversial. These make the best coverlines. Samples of coverlines are: "Christian Rock—Should the Beat Go On?"; "How to Be Your Own Best Friend"; and "How to Teach Your Kids about God."

CROSSOVER MARKET. Some Christian magazines and books also appeal to secular audiences. For example, when books such as those written by Robert Schuller, Charles Colson, and Chuck Swindoll are available in secular bookstores and qualify for the New York Times Bestseller list, they have successfully "crossed over" to markets other than the traditional religious market. Crossover books not only make a lot of money, but also reach a lot of people with their messages.

DOT MATRIX VS. LETTER QUALITY. Of the two types of printers available for use with computers, the letter quality printer produces manuscripts similar to those produced by a typewriter. Many editors refuse to read copy from a dot matrix printer since the letters, created by a series of dots, sometimes are tiring to the eyes. Also, if an optical scanning device is used to read manuscripts, the dot matrix is usually unreadable, since every dot is read as a separate character.

DRAFTS. A draft is one complete version of a story, article or book. A first draft often is called a rough draft and will be subject to much refinement in subsequent drafts.

FAIR USE. Nowhere in the copyright law of 1978 does it say exactly how many words a writer can quote from another writer's work without obtaining permission. A paragraph or two from a book may be "fair use" (be sure and credit the author and the book you're quoting) but even one line of a poem or song could cause legal problems. When in doubt, ask permission.

FILLER. As the name suggests, a filler is a brief item that can be plugged into any hole on a magazine's page to fill up the void. Editors often buy poetry, witty quotes, anecdotes or inspirational incidents to use as fillers. Easy-to-market fillers are those that won't soon be out of date.

FIRST RIGHTS. When an author sells a new manuscript to a publication for use once in a magazine, she or he is selling first rights. After publication, the manuscript can be sold to another editor. This time the writer sells reprint rights or second rights.

FRONTLIST. A publisher's frontlist books are new releases promoted in a current catalog.

GENRE FICTION. Also called category fiction and sometimes, more negatively, "formula" fiction, genre fiction includes romance, mystery, westerns, science fiction, adventure, and the like. The categories are broad and give way to half-breeds: mystery-romance; teen-adventure; Christian historical-romance.

GHOSTWRITER. An author who agrees to write a book or article for someone else is called a ghostwriter. Often he or she is paid a flat fee for the work (usually the advance against royalties), or there may be negotiations for a percentage of sales.

HONORARIUM. Some publications that operate on a limited editorial budget offer contributors a fixed amount of money called an honorarium. It rarely varies regardless of the length or depth of the manuscript.

KILL FEE. If an assigned story, article, poem, or book is canceled by an editor, the writer is paid a portion of the original agreed-to article fee. This portion (often twenty percent) is called a kill fee.

LEAD, HOOK, INTRODUCTION. The opening paragraph(s) of an article or story is called the lead or hook or intro. Its purpose is to grab readers' attention, introduce the topic, establish the tone and mood of the piece.

MS, MSS. These abbreviations for manuscript and

manuscripts (plural) apply to fiction, nonfiction, and poetry. The terms are part of literary lingo, similar to SASE, slush, and the like.

MASS MARKET. A mass market book is not targeted to a specialized audience but has appeal to a very large segment of the reading public.

MASTHEAD. Toward the front of a magazine, near the table of contents, the masthead lists the names and titles of the publication's staff. This list helps the free-lancer know to whom he or she should send his or her query or ms.

MULTIPLE MARKETING. Multiple marketing is the systematic recycling of material to different publications by a free-lance writer. If the author makes only minor changes in a manuscript that has been sold previously, she or he offers "reprint rights" to subsequent editors. If a new slant is chosen, a different lead is created, and fresh quotes are presented, he or she can sell first rights since the manuscript is truly a new property.

MULTIPLE SUBMISSIONS. The practice of sending an identical manuscript to several editors simultaneously is called making multiple submissions. Many editors frown on it unless they are assured that the material has been sent only to publications that do not have overlapping circulations.

NEWS PEG. In an issue-related article, a news peg is the factor that makes a story timely. It ties the article to something currently in the news and of concern to the public.

OFF THE RECORD. In an interview situation, the person being interviewed may share information that is "off the record" or not for publication. The writer (interviewer) should honor the request and not include the information in the story.

ON ACCEPTANCE/ON PUBLICATION. When a writer is paid on acceptance, he or she is issued a check as soon as the ms has been approved for publication by the editor. The alternative is to be paid when the material appears in print, which can be several months (even years) after submission.

OVER THE TRANSOM. This antiquated term refers to mss that arrive unsolicited at an editor's office. The expression is a throwback to the days when mail carriers would heave large envelopes containing mss up and through the small open windows (transoms) above office doors.

PREWRITING ACTIVITIES. Before a writer begins to put words to paper, she or he needs to decide on the purpose, the audience it is intended to reach, the tone that will be used, the desired length, and several possible markets for the work.

PROPOSAL. When trying to sell a book idea to a publisher, an author submits a proposal containing the following elements: a cover letter that explains what the book is about and why the author is qualified to write it; a summary of the book's plot or main points (three to four pages); a table of contents that names each chapter and gives a two-paragraph synopsis of what it contains; two or three sample chapters (they don't have to be in sequence but can be Chapters One, Five, Ten or any others the author prefers).

PSEUDONYM. Often called a pen name, a pseudonym is a name other than an author's legal name that she or he chooses to use as a byline. The author indicates his or her pseudonym by typing it below the title of the manuscript, while the legal name (to whom the check should be written) is typed in the upper left corner of the ms. Some writers are better known by their pen names (Lewis Carroll rather than Charles Dodgson), and some are more recognizable by their legal names even though they occasionally use a pen name (C. S. Lewis wrote under the name of N. W. Clerk).

QUERY. A query is a one-page sales letter sent by a free-lancer to an editor. The purpose is two-fold: first, to sell the editor on an idea for a story or article; second, to sell the editor on the author as the perfect person to write the story or article.

Q AND A FORMAT. Profile articles based on an interview with one person can be written in narrative style or in question-and-answer format. In a Q and A, an introduction explains the background of the interview (where it took place, who asked the questions). A sequence of questions (often printed in boldface or italics) and answers follows.

REPRINT. Particularly in Christian publishing, reprints can be an excellent source of income for the freelancer. Often markets don't overlap, so a writer can sell a story or article to one denominational publication and then sell reprint rights to another denominational publication. In order to do this, a writer must avoid selling all rights to anyone.

ROUND-UP ARTICLE. One of the easiest types of nonfiction to produce is the roundup. The author chooses a timely topic, phrases it in the form of a question, then asks several experts to comment on it.

ROYALTIES. Carefully spelled out in the book contract between writer and publisher, royalties are the monies paid annually or semiannually to the author. Eight to ten percent of a book's retail price is average, although the percentage may increase on a sliding scale after certain sales figures are reached.

SASE. A SASE (self-addressed, stamped envelope) should always accompany any correspondence sent to an editor.

SELF-PUBLISHING. When a writer pays to have a book manuscript put into published form he or she contacts a subsidy publisher (also called a vanity press) and selects the "package" wanted (and affordable). Cost is based on the length of the book; the number of copies printed; the quality of the paper stock, cover, and jacket; the inclusion of photographs and illustrations, and the amount of copy-editing that is needed.

SIDEBAR. A related but separate article, a sidebar presents additional information not contained in the main story. Sidebars are short (500 words or so), have their own titles, and often are placed in boxes or under screens (shaded areas) to make them typographically attractive. Editors like them because they add interest to a magazine page; readers like them because they're quick and easy to absorb. Many readers sample the sidebar first and then turn to the main article (sometimes called the mainbar).

SLUSH. The stacks of unsolicited manuscripts that accumulate in every editorial office are called slush. These submissions generally are read by a first reader who rejects the majority of them and designates a handful for consideration by a second reader.

SOURCE. Any provider of information is called a source. Most writers cultivate many knowledgeable, credible sources whom they can contact when they need to quote experts in a particular field.

SPECULATION. Unless an editor is familiar with an author, she or he may ask the author to work on speculation. This means that the editor is favorably impressed by the author's query and wishes to see the completed ms. However, the editor is under no obligation to buy the ms or to pay a kill fee.

SUBSIDIARY RIGHTS. Successful books sometimes lead to lucrative spin-off products such as movies, paperback versions, and audio cassettes. How the profits from these products will be divided are covered in the book contract under "subsidiary rights." As with any part of the contract, they are open to negotiation.

TEARSHEETS/CLIPS. When considering a query or proposal from a writer, an editor often asks to see samples of the author's previously published works. Newspaper samples are usually cut out (clips), while magazine samples are generally sent in full-page form (tearsheets).

UNSOLICITED MS. Any manuscript that is mailed to an editor without the editor's prior knowledge or invitation is unsolicited. The wise free-lancer writes a query letter to spark interest in the ms before forwarding the completed piece. Some editors refuse to read unsolicited material.

WORK-FOR-HIRE. A work-for-hire agreement, signed by a writer and a publisher, gives all rights (including the right to copyright) to the publishing company. The author may not sell or use her or his material again without written approval of its owner, the publisher.

Notes

Chapter One
1. Alan Lakein, "How to Use Your Time Wisely," *U.S. News and World Report*, (Jan. 19, 1976):45-47.
2. Ken Taylor, "The Man Who Brought the Bible Alive," with Virginia Muir and Matt Price, *Christian Herald*, (July/Aug. 1987):18-21.
3. Holly Miller, "The Total Writer," *Writer's Digest*, (Aug. 1981):24.
4. Holly Miller, "Monday Morning Gospel," *ASCAP in Action*, (Winter 1987):36-37.

Chapter Two
5. Merrill McLoughlin, "America's New Civil War," *U.S. News and World Report*, (Oct. 3, 1988):23-30.
6. Holly Miller, "If Not Abortion, What?" *Christian Herald*, (Jan. 1989):39-44.

Chapter Three
7. David E. Sumner, "Sally Stuart on Getting Published," *Christian Writers Newsletter*, (Oct. 1988):1.

Chapter Four
8. Ralph Daigh, *Maybe You Should Write A Book*, (Englewood Cliffs, N.J.: Prentice-Hall, Inc., 1977):162.
9. Holly Miller, "Life After Breast Cancer," *Today's Christian Woman*, (May/June 1985):44-47.
10. Dennis E. Hensley and Holly G. Miller, *The Gift*, (Harvest House, 1988):16.
11. Holly Miller, "Two's Company," *Today's Christian Woman*, (July/Aug. 1986): 24-27.
12. Holly Miller, "Ethnic Congregations: Melting Pot or Salad Bowl?" *Vital Christianity*, (June 28, 1987):6-7.

13. Holly Miller, "Life After Breast Cancer," *Today's Christian Woman*, (May/June 1985):44.

14. Holly Miller, "Life After Breast Cancer," *Today's Christian Woman*, (May/June 1985):47.

Chapter Five

15. Holly Miller, "And Anna Makes Three," *Christian Herald*, (Dec. 1984):12-15.

Chapter Seven

16. Holly Miller, "Over the Hill with Your Car Top Down," *Today's Christian Woman*, (Jan./Feb. 1989):58-59.

Chapter Eight

17. Alan Freeman, "You May Not Know His Names," *Wall Street Journal*, (Jan. 12, 1987):1.

18. Alan Freeman, "A Title Can Make a Difference," *Wall Street Journal*, (Jan. 16, 1989):B-1.

Chapter Ten

19. John Newland, "Split Infinitive to Slowly Become Acceptable," *Indiana Alumni*, (Jan./Feb. 1989):56.

20. Speech by James Kilpatrick, (University of Notre Dame, (Aug. 1985).

21. James Kilpatrick, "The Writer's Art," *Indianapolis Star*, (Jan. 15, 1989).

22. "Surveying the State of the Lingo," *Time*, (Nov. 2, 1987):55.

23. "Words Win Dishonorable Mention," *Associated Press*, (Jan. 2, 1988).

Chapter Eleven

24. William Griffin, "2000, an Extraordinary Year!!" *Publishers Weekly*, (March 4, 1988):40-41.

25. Donald Murray, *Writing For Your Readers*, (the Globe Pequod Press, 1983):21.

Chapter Twelve

26. Column by Leonard Felder, *Publishers Weekly*, (Aug. 28, 1987):23-24.